THE EASY 5-INGREDIENT VEGAN COOKBOOK

THE EASY
5-Ingredient
VEGAN
COOKBOOK

100 Healthy Plant-Based Recipes

NANCY MONTUORI, Ordinary Vegan

Photography by Thomas J. Story

ROCKRIDGE
PRESS

For general information on our other products and services or to obtain technical support, please contact our Customer Care Department within the United States at (866) 744-2665, or outside the United States at (510) 253-0500.

Rockridge Press publishes its books in a variety of electronic and print formats. Some content that appears in print may not be available in electronic books, and vice versa.

Interior and Cover Designer: Julie Gueraseva
Art Producer: Sara Feinstein
Editor: Myryah Irby
Photography © 2019 Thomas J Story
Food Styling by Karen Shinto
Author photo courtesy of © Amanda Gallant

ISBN: Print 978-1-64152-988-4 | eBook 978-1-64152-989-1
R0

———

This book is dedicated to John Montuori—my hard-working, blue-collar, Italian father—for teaching me the meaning of a strong work ethic and kindness. I would not be who I am or where I am today without his inspiration and guidance.

———

Contents

CHAPTER 8: STAPLES AND SAUCES 149

CHAPTER 9: SWEETS 171

Introduction

MY DECISION TO EAT PLANT-BASED was an unplanned, serendipitous event that ended up changing every aspect of my life. At a young age, I contracted a disease that landed me in the hospital for six months inside an iron lung. When I was released from the hospital, I needed daily therapeutic exercise to restore movement to my limbs. My family couldn't afford physical therapists, so my care fell into the hands of my loving aunts, cousins, and godparents. I credit their diligent physical therapy for my ability to fully heal and walk again.

My illness has had a powerful impact on my life, and I have always strived to eat healthily and take care of my body. I never wanted to be sick again. Unfortunately, I fell victim to our government's food pyramid, false advertising, and the latest food trends. I was taught that I needed to drink cow's milk to get strong bones and to eat meat to get protein. I was following dietary recommendations from people I trusted, but these recommendations were actually hurting my health and well-being.

On May 1, 2011, I went to see the documentary film *Forks Over Knives*. After watching that movie, I was convinced of the connection between animal protein and disease. From that day forward, I adopted a plant-based lifestyle.

In a short period, I was able to discontinue my statin medication for high cholesterol, and my energy level was sky high. Those were just a couple of the immediate health benefits. I also felt lighter, brighter, and more connected to everything I did. This incredible feeling of well-being made me want to share my experience with the world, and I began writing my blog, Ordinary Vegan. In 2013 I became certified in plant-based nutrition and dedicated my existence to helping people live a long and healthy life.

Before I became vegan, I never thought about the impact my diet had on animals and the climate. In the United States alone, 10 billion animals a year are being killed to put food on our plates, according to data found on the Animal Clock website. It's become such a big business that the majority of these animals are subjected to extreme discomfort and pain in the name of efficiency.

Animal agriculture is also choking the planet. As noted by Climate Nexus, it is the second-largest contributor to human-made greenhouse gas emissions, and a leading cause of deforestation and water and air pollution. Greenhouse gas emissions cause a greenhouse effect that traps us inside and changes the temperature of the Earth's surface. When the world's temperature rises, it leads to more droughts, fires, warmer oceans, melting glaciers, rising sea levels, and changing rain and snow patterns.

Last but not least, what we eat can make us ill. In 2015, the World Health Organization announced that 8 ounces of processed meat a day could raise the risk of colon cancer by a whopping 18 percent. Dairy has also been linked to cancer. Biochemist and author of *The China Study*, Dr. T. Colin Campbell, called casein, the main protein in cow's milk, "the most relevant cancer promoter found in the last 50 years." Cow's milk and products from cow's milk, like cheese, are also the top source of saturated fat in the American diet, contributing to heart disease, obesity, and type 2 diabetes, according to research from the Physicians Committee for Responsible Medicine.

As news of the health and environmental benefits spreads, more people are switching to a plant-based lifestyle. Between 2014 and 2017, the number of US consumers identifying as vegan grew to 6 percent from 1 percent (a 600 percent increase), according to analytics company GlobalData. That's still a pretty small portion, but plant-based food has moved into the mainstream.

The business of providing plant-based meals is also booming. Vegan options now exist in some of the largest fast-food chains in the United States, from Subway to McDonald's. Although there are many fast-food and processed vegan options now available, that does not mean they are healthy. The biggest health benefits come from a clean, unprocessed, whole-food, plant-based diet. Just because it's vegan doesn't mean it's healthy.

Processed vegan food may contain all the unhealthy oils, fats, artificial ingredients, and chemicals that are best avoided in any diet. This book is dedicated to providing you with minimally processed, nutritious recipes that include the five main food groups essential for a healthy whole foods diet. Each recipe uses just five ingredients—not counting the basic staples of salt, black pepper, fresh garlic, fresh onions, vegetable broth, and olive oil. All of these recipes can be enhanced by a squeeze of citrus, a sprinkling of seeds, or one of the many sauces included in this book.

Whether you're new to plant-based eating or have fully adopted the lifestyle, I welcome you and hope this cookbook can help you on your journey. A compassionate life begins with what you put on your plate.

CHAPTER 1

A Plant-Based Blueprint for Healthy Eating

I'm always asked how to begin a vegan diet. There is no easy answer, and an easy answer is never the truth. Big transformations in life take time and commitment, but they also have a massive impact on those who choose to make them. Eating plant-based brings physical changes, improved health, and more energy. And the transformation goes well beyond physical outcomes.

Aristotle said the soul is not an independently existing substance, and that it's linked directly to the body. So when the body feels strong, the soul will, too. A strong soul is more connected to everything that exists in life.

When you're transitioning to a plant-based lifestyle, keep your goal in mind and find a strategy that works for you. If you feel giving up all animal-based foods at once works, then do it. If you need more time to adjust to a plant-based diet, just take it slowly and start gradually eliminating nonvegan foods. Eat what you love; just find vegan alternatives. Although I recommend cutting down on processed foods, try a vegan version at first: If you miss chicken, try vegan chicken. If you miss old-fashioned burgers, try a plant-based option. Make the changes you feel comfortable with at your own pace.

Most important, you don't need to spend hours in the kitchen or buy expensive ingredients to create delicious, satisfying, interesting plant-based meals. I wrote this book to make it as convenient as possible for you to add more plant-based meals to your life without a fuss—as well as show you how delicious food can taste without animal protein.

Many of us eat on the run. It's a lot easier than you think to order vegan meals at nonvegan restaurants. It just takes some time to adjust and learn what to order. Most restaurants will accommodate you and cook your food without animal products. The first thing I do at restaurants is look at the side dishes. Often I will build my entire meal around them.

The last challenge I want to address is acceptance. Being the only vegan in your family or circle of friends can be tricky. My recommendation is to just be a shining example of health, wellness, energy, and compassion. And take it from me, it won't be long before your friends and family want to have that same experience.

Plant-Based Eating Made Simple

Whether you are trying to eat plants full time or simply looking to integrate more into your diet, I want to help you hit the ground running by providing you with all the information you need for maximum health and wellness—and convenience. Eating more plant-based meals doesn't need to be complicated.

Every recipe in this book will be the blueprint for crafting a nutritious, easy meal. Although these recipes contain only five ingredients (not counting a few basic staples), I want to encourage you to think more like a chef. Consider how you can maximize the flavor of each ingredient. Whether it is roasting, caramelization, grilling, toasting, or adding crunch, don't be afraid to experiment. Cooking is an opportunity to be creative.

My goal is to provide you with as many nutrients as I can pack into a simple five-ingredient plant-based blueprint recipe, but it is up to you to build out from that with sides of vegetables, fruits, grains, legumes, and healthy fats. Try to eat a leafy green every day and choose fresh fruit for dessert, baked to intensify the sweet, vibrant flavors. Add some power boosters, too—for example, 2 tablespoons of hemp seeds daily for omega-3 fatty acids.

To simplify your vegan lifestyle, plan what you want to eat. Planning saves time and money, and it allows for a lot of flexibility and variation in your weekly meals. When possible, try to batch cook (cook more than you need at one time so you have some basics to use throughout the week). Make a pot of beans or some grains and steam some vegetables and keep them in the refrigerator for quick healthy meals. Planning your meals will also help you make fewer trips to the supermarket.

When in doubt, remember the vegan power plate. Just evenly divide your plate into the four nutritious food groups: fruits, vegetables, grains, and legumes. Then top with a small portion of healthy fats, such as nuts, seeds, or avocado slices. You can use this vegan power plate to create soups, stews, salads, or a simple dish of food. It's that easy.

Although you don't need a lot of fancy kitchen equipment for the recipes in this book, I do highly recommend having a food processor. While blenders have become more capable over the years, they still don't do much more than blend. Food processors are easily the most versatile kitchen appliance you can buy. You can use them to slice vegetables, chop, grate, make hummus and pesto, turn whole grains into flour, chop nuts, purée soups, and create nut-based sauces. Also, capable models aren't too expensive.

Finally, never believe you have to be a perfect vegan. Every plant-based meal you eat is a powerful display of compassion to your body, the environment, and animals.

Powerful Proteins

The most common misconception about protein is that you have to eat meat, dairy, and eggs to meet your protein needs. The truth is that it's easy to get enough of this nutrient without eating animal products. You can meet all your protein needs simply by eating a well-rounded, whole-food, plant-based diet.

For example, did you know one cup of cooked sweet potato contains 5 grams of protein? Or that 1 cup of peas contains more than 8 grams of protein? Did you know broccoli contains more protein per calorie than steak? A typical plant-based diet contains plenty of protein. One of my favorite sources of protein is hemp seeds. They contain more than 6 grams of protein per tablespoon, including the nine essential amino acids that your body can't make.

The second misconception about protein is that you need to eat a lot of it. However, if you look at the studies from the World Health Organization's Food and Agricultural Organization and *The China Study*, you only need about 8 to 10 percent of total calorie consumption to come from protein. If you follow the traditional Western diet of meat and dairy products, you are likely getting two to three times as much protein as your body needs.

Furthermore, when animal protein intake increases to levels above 10 percent, disease risk also increases, according to research in a study in *Cell Metabolism*. Extra protein is not used efficiently by the body and may impose a metabolic burden on the bones, kidneys, and liver. Moreover, a study published in *JAMA Internal Medicine* found that diets high in animal protein are also associated with increased risk for heart disease and cancer, due to the excess saturated fat and cholesterol.

The idea that plant proteins are incomplete and that you have to combine specific foods is another myth that won't go away. First, the concept that plant protein is inferior to animal protein was debunked by the scientific nutrition community decades ago. You don't need one protein to complement another to get enough protein, because your body maintains pools of free amino acids that can do all the complementing for you.

Above all, eating a wide variety of healthy plant-based foods will provide you with all the protein you need without the health risks of eating meat, eggs, and dairy, and you can still enjoy many of your favorite flavors and recipes by replacing the animal protein with plant protein. For example, I still make my mother's beef stew recipe, but I replaced the beef with seitan, which has a chewy, dense flavor that resembles meat.

Here are some other easy swaps.

ANIMAL PROTEIN	VEGAN SWAP	PROTEIN PER 6-OUNCE SERVING	BONUS NUTRIENTS
Beef	Seitan	42 grams	Iron
Beef	Tempeh	31 grams	Iron, potassium, calcium
Beef	Portobello mushrooms	6 grams	Fiber, vitamin C, iron, magnesium
Chicken	Chickpeas	32 grams	Vitamin C, vitamin B6, calcium, magnesium
Chicken	Tofu	14 grams	Iron, calcium, magnesium
Beef burger	Lentils	15 grams	Fiber, iron
Beef chili	Black bean chili	10 grams	Fiber, calcium, potassium

The bottom line is that foods derived from plants lack the cholesterol that animal protein contains, and provide you with an array of nutrients that you can only get from plants, such as phytochemicals, fiber, beta carotene, and vitamin C.

Healthy Fats

When it comes to your health, plant-based fats are superior to animal-based fats. Ounce for ounce, they pack more nutrients into fewer calories, plus they contain essential dietary fiber that animal-based fats do not.

The main difference between healthy fat and unhealthy fat is the way it affects your "good" (HDL) and "bad" (LDL) cholesterol levels. Studies now show that eating polyunsaturated and monounsaturated fats can help lower your bad cholesterol and reduce your risk of heart disease. Polyunsaturated fat is found mostly in plant-based foods. Monounsaturated fats are found in high-fat fruits such as olives and avocados.

Here is a list of my favorite plant-based fats. I recommend making them 10 to 15 percent of your overall diet.

AVOCADOS: Avocados are loaded with heart-healthy monounsaturated fatty acids. Monounsaturated fats not only reduce bad cholesterol levels, but they also provide a good source of the antioxidant vitamin E, a nutrient often lacking in American diets.

CACAO NIBS: Cacao nibs are small pieces of crushed cocoa beans that have been fermented and dried. They are rich in so many minerals and packed with antioxidants, even outranking blueberries. Cacao consumption can also benefit people with blood sugar control issues.

CASHEWS: Known for their buttery, creamy taste, cashews are a great base for many plant-based recipes in this book. And they are also an incredible source of vitamins and minerals, including vitamins E, K, and B6. The fat in cashews helps you feel full and may help manage weight.

GROUND FLAXSEED: One tablespoon of ground flaxseed contains 2 grams of polyunsaturated fatty acids, including omega-3s. Omega-3 fatty acids are essential nutrients for good health and can reduce triglycerides in your blood, which reduces your risk of heart disease.

HEMP SEEDS: They're rich in healthy fats, but the real value of hemp seeds is that they contain all 20 known amino acids, including the nine essential amino acids our bodies cannot produce. This makes them a complete protein. Because we cannot produce these amino acids, we must eat them in our diet. I recommend 2 tablespoons a day.

SOYBEANS: Soy often gets a bad rap, but soybeans are a good source of polyunsaturated fat and are almost 40 percent protein. Soy is also a complete protein and contains the nine essential amino acids our bodies can't produce. My favorite sources of soy are edamame, miso, soy sauce, tempeh, and tofu.

WALNUTS: All nuts are packed with good fats, protein, minerals, and vitamins. But walnuts contain the highest level of antioxidants compared to other nuts. Antioxidants protect your cells against the effects of free radicals—substances that are linked to aging and a host of diseases.

Carbohydrates

There is a great deal of misunderstanding about carbohydrates and diet. An ideal diet for humans is 80 percent carbohydrate, 10 percent protein, and 10 percent fat, according to nutritional scientist and author of *The China Study* Dr. T. Colin Campbell. Carbohydrates are quickly metabolized and used as the body's primary source of energy, so they are essential fuel. Also, the brain, kidneys, muscles, and heart all need carbohydrates to function properly.

It's best to choose carbohydrates that are naturally rich in fiber. Foods that fall into that category are plant foods: legumes, grains, vegetables, fruits, and healthy fats like nuts and seeds. Refined carbohydrates, such as white bread and white pasta, are forms of sugars and starches that don't exist in nature. They do come from whole, natural foods, but they have been altered in some way by processing to refine them. The process of refining food not only removes the fiber, it also removes much of the food's nutritional value. Refined carbohydrates can raise insulin levels and can promote obesity when combined with fat.

The carbohydrates in whole foods have the opposite effect. Because of the natural fiber in the foods, these carbs get absorbed slowly into the system, avoiding spikes in blood sugar levels. Whole-grain unprocessed carbohydrates are filled with healthy complex carbs, fiber, protein, vitamins, and minerals. Healthy plant-based carbs are not the enemy in the war on carbohydrates.

Eating the Rainbow

You can learn a lot about your food just by its color. Fruits and vegetables fall into five color categories: purple/blue, red, green, orange, and white/brown. Each vibrant color carries its own unique set of disease-fighting nutrients called phytochemicals—natural chemicals that are *only available in plants*. They are responsible for the color, flavor, and aroma of plant foods.

There are more than 25,000 of these nonessential nutrients. That means the human body does not require them for sustaining life, but over the years, scientific research has discovered that phytochemicals can protect humans against many chronic diseases, including cancer, Alzheimer's disease, and heart disease. So let's break it down.

BLUE AND PURPLE

Blueberries, eggplant, purple beets, purple cauliflower, purple grapes, purple yams.

This brilliant, color-saturated group gets their color from anthocyanin, a type of antioxidant flavonoid. The outstanding players are blueberries, purple grapes, and purple yams. Blueberries have a large amount of antioxidants. Purple grapes have resveratrol, which protects the body against damage that can put you at a higher risk for cancer and heart disease.

RED

Cherries, raspberries, red apples, red beets, red bell peppers, red grapes, red onions, rhubarb, strawberries, tomatoes, watermelon.

This group gets its rich color from lycopene, which has been found to reduce the risk of cancer and protect from the harmful effects of pollution. The outstanding players are strawberries, watermelon, and red bell peppers. One cup of strawberries provides 89 milligrams of vitamin C, or 99 percent of the vitamin C you need each day. Watermelon contains citrulline, an amino acid that can increase nitric oxide levels in the body. Nitric oxide helps your blood vessels expand, which lowers blood pressure. Red peppers are one of the healthiest foods you can eat; they are incredibly high in vitamin C and vitamin A.

ORANGE AND YELLOW

Cantaloupe, carrots, corn, golden beets, lemons, mangos, oranges, peaches, pineapple, pumpkin, sweet potatoes.

Carotenoids give this sun-loving group their vibrant color. Carotenoids are beneficial antioxidants that can enhance your immune system and protect you from chronic disease. Lutein is one of 600 known naturally occurring carotenoids. It is often called the eye vitamin because it's an essential nutrient for healthy vision. The outstanding players in this group are oranges and carrots. Oranges are well known for their vitamin C content, a potent antioxidant that can protect cells from harmful free radicals. Oranges also contain health-promoting compounds called flavanones. These citrus phytochemicals are associated with a reduced risk of certain chronic diseases, including cardiovascular disease, atherosclerosis, and cancer. They support and enhance the body's defenses against oxidative stress. Carrots are the most abundant vegetable source of beta carotene, which is converted to vitamin A within the body. Health benefits of vitamin A include maintaining healthy teeth, bones, and white blood cells, and promoting a healthy immune system, good eye health, and healthy skin.

GREEN

Avocados, broccoli, Brussels sprouts, collard greens, edamame, green apples, green grapes, kale, kiwis, peas, spinach.

This group gets its color from chlorophyll, which has vitamins, antioxidants, and therapeutic properties. Studies have shown that chlorophyll decreases the risk of developing cancer because it cleanses the liver. It is also a potent anti-inflammatory and has been found to speed up wound healing and protect the skin. The outstanding green player award goes to spinach, which has the highest chlorophyll content: 1 cup contains 23 milligrams.

WHITE AND BROWN

Bananas, cauliflower, Jerusalem artichokes, jicama, mushrooms, onions, parsnips, shallots, turnips, white peaches, white potatoes.

They may not be the brightest of the rainbow, but these foods contain fiber, potassium, and magnesium, all of which support a healthy immune system. The outstanding players in this group are mushrooms, bananas, and artichokes. For example, 1 cup of raw chopped mushrooms has 3 grams of protein, 350 milligrams of potassium, and only 21 calories. Potassium helps your muscles work properly, including the heart muscle. Bananas and white potatoes are great sources of potassium. One medium artichoke has some of the highest levels of antioxidants and fiber of any vegetable. Fiber is best known for helping keep food moving efficiently through the body. It also stabilizes blood sugar levels, reduces the absorption of cholesterol into the bloodstream, and prevents fats from being absorbed.

Unquestionably, the variety of vitamins, minerals, antioxidants, phytochemicals, and fiber in plants have enormous healing powers.

Stocking Your Vegan Pantry

A well-stocked pantry will enable you to get a nutritious meal on the table in minutes. This book is about maximum flavor with minimum ingredients, and I want to introduce you to those ingredients so you feel confident cooking with them. The foods here are in addition to the fresh fruits and vegetables you'll be buying weekly.

ESSENTIALS

Let's start with the staples that are so basic, they won't even count in the five ingredients in each recipe. These staples appear in black within the list of ingredients:

LOW-SODIUM ORGANIC VEGETABLE BROTH AND EXTRA-VIRGIN OLIVE OIL: What has 120 calories per tablespoon and is 100 percent fat? The answer is oil. And when I say oil, I mean any oil: coconut oil, olive oil, vegetable oil, palm oil. Besides avoiding meat and dairy, cutting back on oil is an essential component of a healthy diet. Although this isn't an oil-free cookbook, most of the recipes give you the option of using low-sodium vegetable broth instead of oil to sauté, roast, and caramelize. But the choice is yours. If you suffer from heart disease, I do recommend an oil-free plant-based diet.

VEGETABLE BROTH is a key flavor-building component of the best vegan cooking, but quality is essential. Always look for vegetable broth that is low-sodium and has a minimum of ingredients other than actual vegetables. All it needs to have is carrot, onion, celery, leeks, mushrooms, or tomatoes, and a few herbs. Buy organic vegetable broth that is guaranteed to be free of pesticides and genetically modified organisms (GMOs). You can also make your own. I like to save vegetable scraps in a big bag in the freezer and when I have a full bag, I add them to water. Simmer for 30 minutes, strain, and you have fresh vegetable broth.

Sautéing with vegetable broth instead of oil is simple. Just add ¼ to ⅓ cup of vegetable broth to a pan and heat over medium heat. Add your vegetables, stirring occasionally, and add more broth if needed to keep the food from sticking to the pan.

FRESH GARLIC AND ONIONS: My motto is, where onion goes, garlic follows. Many of the recipes in this cookbook draw on the deep savory aroma and flavor of onions and garlic, so keep plenty on hand. White and yellow onions and garlic can last up to two to three months when stored separately in a cool, dry, well-ventilated place, so you can buy them in bulk and always have them available. Keeping both of these produce items out of the refrigerator will improve their quality and shelf life. Garlic is a flavor powerhouse and highly nutritious. It tastes best if it's cooked quickly, about 30 seconds, over medium heat. Burnt garlic has a distinct, bitter, and unpleasant taste, so never overcook it.

SALT AND FRESHLY GROUND BLACK PEPPER: Salt is the most basic of seasonings, but adding too much salt can be unhealthy. I recommend adding a small amount of salt during cooking or salting in the end after tasting, to avoid oversalting. Keep in mind that kosher salt and some sea salts have larger crystal sizes than table salt and may make salt measurements inaccurate. As far as pepper goes, a fresh grind of pepper releases incredible flavor, so a pepper mill is worth the investment.

VEGAN BASICS

These are items that I use throughout this cookbook. They help maximize food's flavor and nutrition and are common staples for a plant-based kitchen. A few of the recipes also call for vegan mayonnaise and vegan sour cream. I recommend you make your own, and I have included recipes for them in this book. But if you use store-bought occasionally, don't worry. Always remember, a little goes a long way.

Plant-Based Proteins

CANNED COOKED BEANS: Beans like chickpeas, black beans, and cannellini are nutritious, versatile, inexpensive, and a great source of protein. From chili and soup to burritos, canned cooked beans can become a delicious meal in minutes. Also, the liquid from cooked chickpeas contains aquafaba. This starchy liquid is a great binder and egg replacer, so always save it. It will last two or three days in the refrigerator. Always purchase non-BPA cans.

JACKFRUIT: Jackfruit is from a tree in the mulberry family that is native to parts of India, Asia, East Africa, and Brazil. Quite unique and tasty, jackfruit is rich in energy, dietary fiber, minerals, and vitamins, yet contains no saturated fats or cholesterol. Like tofu, it makes a good base for other flavors. Many vegetarians consider it a great substitute for meat because of its texture and chewy flavor. You can now find it at most mainstream health food stores, and Asian and Caribbean grocery stores. It comes in cans and vacuum-packed. Make sure you buy the "young green" not-quite-ripe fruit. There is another type called "ripe," which is canned in syrup and mainly used in sweet dishes.

TEMPEH: Although tempeh isn't quite as popular as tofu, it is a powerhouse protein mainstay of many vegan diets. Tempeh is made from fermented soybeans bound together into a cake. Tempeh can be used on practically everything from salads to sandwiches, and even as a vegan bacon replacement. Tempeh is also high in protein—1 cup provides 31 grams.

TOFU: Tofu is high in protein, low in fat, and one of my favorite plant-based proteins. It can be baked, sautéed, marinated, and scrambled. Sometimes soy products like tofu get a bad rap. The most common misconception about soy is that it contains estrogen. It does not. Estrogen is a hormone found in animals and does not occur in plants. Rather, soy contains phytoestrogens, and these mimic some of the actions of estrogen. Soy is the cornerstone of a traditional Asian diet, and Asian populations have historically had lower rates of chronic disease.

SEITAN: Seitan is a popular vegan substitute for meat that's made from the gluten that has been separated from starch and the other components in flour. Vegans and vegetarians allergic to soy often use seitan as their meat substitute. Seitan is also well known for its texture, which is more similar to meat than tofu and tempeh. It absorbs flavor well, and I love using it in stews, tacos, and stir-fries. Bottom line, you can use this protein the same way you would cook any animal protein.

Fruits and Vegetables

CANNED TOMATOES: Although fresh tomatoes are supremely delicious, they are only in season in the summer, and out-of-season tomatoes often lack flavor. Canned tomatoes are a healthy alternative to fresh tomatoes and add a deep, rich, tangy flavor to many soups and stews.

FROZEN FRUITS AND VEGETABLES: It can be hard to keep fresh fruits and vegetables on hand, and frozen is a great alternative. Fruits and vegetables are picked and frozen at the peak of their ripeness, and studies show they hold on to all of their nutrients. In fact, many frozen fruits and vegetables retain more nutrients when they are frozen compared to fresh. Never hesitate to stock up on frozen organic fruits and vegetables. Organic corn, peas, and spinach can come in handy for a quick stir-fry or stew. Add frozen fruits to smoothies.

Nuts and Seeds

CHIA SEEDS: These are considered one of the healthiest and most beneficial foods on the planet. They deliver a massive amount of nutrients. A 1-ounce serving of chia seeds contains 11 grams of fiber and 4 grams of protein. They are an excellent source of omega-3 fatty acids, are rich in antioxidants, and provide fiber, iron, and calcium. Adding them to a dish is a quick and easy way to add energy to your day. Many health experts believe that chia seeds can aid in weight loss because their soluble fiber absorbs large amounts of water and expands in your stomach, which increases fullness and slows food absorption.

HEMP SEEDS: The beauty of hemp seeds is that they are a complete protein, containing all nine essential amino acids our bodies cannot provide. Hemp seeds also provide more protein than flaxseed or chia seeds, and no other food contains the ideal ratio of omega-3 and omega-6 fats like the mighty hemp seed. Enjoy hemp seeds sprinkled on top of beans, greens, salads, or mixed into your morning oatmeal. They are delicious and have a pleasant, nutty taste.

ROASTED PUMPKIN SEEDS: Also known as pepitas, these seeds are rich in manganese and potassium, which, in addition to all their health benefits, can help with anxiety. They are also a good source of zinc, which is essential for brain and nerve development.

SESAME SEEDS: These seeds are a little sweet and a little nutty. Sesame seeds provide healthy fats and essential amino acids, and are a great source of B vitamins, fiber, and minerals including iron, zinc, magnesium, and manganese.

TAHINI: Tahini is a type of sauce or paste made from ground sesame seeds and is one of the main ingredients in hummus.

Grains and Breads

GRAINS: Everyone has their favorite grains, but I particularly love quinoa and farro for their high protein content. Quinoa is also a complete protein.

WHOLE-WHEAT TORTILLAS: Tortillas freeze well and thaw quickly. Keep them handy for a quick taco or bake them to make healthy chips for dips.

Dairy Alternatives

LIGHT COCONUT MILK: Coconut milk is the liquid pressed from the grated flesh of a fresh, ripe coconut. It can add a flavorful, creamy quality to soups and stews. Look for organic varieties packed in non-BPA cans.

UNSWEETENED PLANT MILK: I love unsweetened almond milk, but there are many plant-based nondairy milks to choose from. Check the labels first to make sure they don't contain added sugar. If a recipe in one of your nonvegan cookbooks calls for buttermilk, combine 1 tablespoon of apple cider vinegar with 1 cup of nondairy milk and let sit for five to 10 minutes to curdle.

Flavor Boosters

DIJON MUSTARD: Dijon is the secret ingredient in countless sauces. It adds a pungent flavor with few calories and can unlock the full potential of many dishes.

FERMENTED FOODS: Sauerkraut and kimchi are examples of probiotic fermented foods. Probiotics protect against digestive disorders and can play a role in cancer prevention. Eat some right out of the jar, add a forkful to your salads, or layer them on a sandwich.

GINGER: Chopped or grated, fresh ginger is a clean, spicy, flavor enhancer that also has numerous healing properties. Ginger has a long history of aiding in digestion; it contains a digestive enzyme called zingibain that helps the body break down protein, and aids in relieving stomach upset or nausea. Ginger's pungent components also have powerful anti-inflammatory and antioxidant activities, making it useful if you suffer from arthritis.

HOT SAUCE: Hot peppers have a compound called capsaicin, which has metabolism-boosting properties and contains many impressive health benefits. A dash of hot sauce can add a lot of flavor to a dish. You will find sriracha sauce—an Asian chili paste—in some of the recipes here, but feel free to substitute whatever kind of hot sauce you prefer. And turn up the heat if that suits you.

LEMONS AND LIMES: Citrus can be stored in the refrigerator crisper drawer for weeks, so don't be afraid to stock up. A simple squeeze of juice or dash of zest can heighten other flavors, and add a bright, tangy taste to foods.

NUTRITIONAL YEAST: Nutritional yeast is a deactivated yeast, which means the yeast cells are killed during processing and are inactive in the final product. A single tablespoon contains 4 grams of protein, with all nine essential amino acids. Nutritional yeast has a cheesy, nutty, umami-rich flavor. It can add a richness to soups and gravies and makes a perfect cheese replacement. Sprinkle nutritional yeast on anything you'd typically top with Parmesan cheese.

ORGANIC PURE MAPLE SYRUP: Maple syrup is one of the pricier items on the list, but it's worth every penny. When buying maple syrup, make sure to read the label carefully and be sure you get real maple syrup, not just maple-flavored syrup. Pure maple syrup, tapped from trees, undergoes less processing than refined sugars. It also contains antioxidants and minerals like zinc and potassium.

ORGANIC PURE VANILLA EXTRACT: Vanilla plays a delicious role in sweet goods by enhancing all the other flavors in the recipe. It's wonderful added to smoothies, too. Make sure you buy pure vanilla extract, which contains vanillin, a compound derived from real vanilla beans. Imitation vanilla can contain many artificial ingredients and alcohol to preserve flavor. Always stick with pure vanilla and look for "vanilla bean" on the label's ingredient list, with no added corn syrup or sugar.

LOW-SODIUM SOY SAUCE OR TAMARI: Soy sauce is an incredibly versatile ingredient that adds a wide range of flavor to a variety of dishes. It's made from fermented soybeans and is packed with satisfying, savory, umami flavors. Many people choose tamari instead of soy sauce because most brands are wheat-free, which makes them safer for a gluten-free diet. Tamari is also fermented, which makes it smoother, richer, and less salty than typical soy sauce.

VINEGAR: Vinegar brings brightness and contrast to many dishes. Balsamic vinegar is one of the most popular varieties, and can lend complex flavors, including a sour sweetness, to a simple dish. A quality balsamic can make all the difference. Much like wine, real balsamic is aged, which is why true balsamic vinegars can be expensive. When deciding which one to buy, look at the ingredients label; it should be at least 12 years old.

Mild vinegars include white wine vinegar, champagne vinegar, and rice vinegar. Bold, sharp vinegars include red wine vinegar, apple cider vinegar, and sherry vinegar. Mirin is a sweetened rice wine vinegar and can add sweetness and flavor to many dishes and sauces. I recommend beginning with at least five types of vinegar: white wine, apple cider, balsamic, sherry, and rice wine.

WHITE MISO: Miso is made from fermented soybeans and adds a savory, sweet, and rich flavor to a variety of dishes. Because miso is made of fermented soybeans, it contains lots of enzymes and beneficial bacteria called probiotics, which improve digestion and help maintain gut health.

Dried Herbs and Spices

All herbs and spices add flavor, and many also provide excellent nutrition. Some even have anti-inflammatory properties and provide powerful antioxidants. Here is a list of the dried spices used often in this book. I am sure you already have many of these in your pantry. This list could go on forever, so buy spice blends that fit your favorite flavor profiles.

BASIL: This is a natural adaptogen, which helps your body deal with stress. It is also a rich source of iron, manganese, and vitamins C, A, and K.

CAYENNE PEPPER: This fiery spice contains the powerful compound capsaicin, which has been linked to lower blood pressure and may help relieve pain. Capsaicin also contains metabolism-boosting properties that can assist in weight loss.

CHILI POWDER: This is an excellent antioxidant due to the vitamin C. Chili powder also stimulates the release of endorphins that act as a natural pain killer.

CHINESE FIVE SPICE POWDER: This robust sweet and spicy seasoning mix is used in Chinese cooking. It can add a ton of flavor to any dish.

CINNAMON: This fragrant, warm, sweet spice is high in the compound cinnamaldehyde. Scientists believe this compound is responsible for most of cinnamon's powerful health effects, including antioxidants that may reduce inflammation.

CRUSHED RED PEPPER FLAKES: These add sharp, spicy flavor without overpowering your taste buds with heat. Always use sparingly.

CUMIN: Cumin promotes digestion and contains antibacterial properties. It also aids in respiratory support.

CURRY POWDER: This is a beautiful blend of Indian spices with considerable antibacterial benefits.

MUSTARD: Ground mustard seeds are an excellent source of selenium, which assists with cognitive function and fertility.

OREGANO: This is a bold herb with potent antioxidant and antibacterial properties.

PAPRIKA: This spice has a fragrant, colorful, smoky-sweet flavor.

ROSEMARY: Featuring woodsy aromas of lemon and pine, this herb can help with digestion.

SAFFRON THREADS: These can be pricey, but a few strands go a long way. Saffron is known as a powerful antioxidant and can elevate any meal's taste and appearance.

THYME: This herb has a subtle aroma and a slightly minty flavor. It is packed with vitamin C.

TURMERIC: This yellow spice contains curcumin, which is a powerful antioxidant that can help fight inflammation in the body.

Building Flavor

The recipes in this book provide a basic five-ingredient blueprint for healthy, delicious, plant-based recipes. But there are many ways to build flavors. The more you learn about and include the five tastes in your dishes, the more satisfying your meals will be. These five flavors are bitter, salty, sweet, sour, and pungent/savory (also known as umami).

A great recipe will never contain just one flavor. For example, pair spicy with sweet, like spicy arugula with sweet fennel. Or create a sweet and sour sauce, which is just a sweet component like maple syrup and a sour element like rice vinegar, and a splash of soy sauce and ketchup for umami.

Teach yourself to be a better cook by understanding the importance of acids, such as vinegar and citrus, which play many roles in building and balancing flavors in a dish. A splash of vinegar or a squeeze of lemon can add brightness to a dish and help highlight other flavors. Acids can also work as tenderizers by breaking down fibers in food.

In addition to acids, many people are surprised to learn that it's easy to cook fantastic food without oil or butter. Often I enjoy creating oil-free dressings because they are easy to prepare. A simple combination of an acid like lemon juice, a whole-food fat like nuts or avocado, a sweet element like maple syrup, and spices can create new, exciting flavor profiles. A rich, oil-free creamy dressing or vinaigrette is not just for salads; it can be used to dress up any hot or cold dish.

I also recommend having lots of umami flavor-builders on hand. Miso, soy, nutritional yeast, mushrooms, grilled vegetables, and pickled and fermented foods can add a rich and savory flavor to any dish. Your palette will appreciate them because there are receptors on the tongue that love umami flavors.

When a dish calls for seeds, dry toast them first to bring out more flavor. Simply toast the seeds in a dry, heavy skillet over medium heat for 1 to 2 minutes. You can also dry roast nuts that way. I prefer to toast nuts in the oven. Preheat the oven to 350°F and spread the nuts in an even layer on a baking sheet. Bake for about 5 to 10 minutes, depending on the density of the nut. Good toasted nuts should be fragrant, never burnt. Always give your baking pan a solid shake halfway through for even browning and keep a watchful eye to avoid burning.

Another easy way to enhance the flavor of the food you prepare is by adding fresh herbs or spices. Above all, the goal is to look at every technique of cooking that can take an ingredient to the next flavor level and apply it to your food.

How to Use This Book

When I was presented with the challenge of developing 100 plant-based recipes, each with only five main ingredients, I was hesitant at first. But then I realized one of the most common barriers to eating plant-based foods is the learning curve and the time it takes to cook, and I want to make things easy and delicious for you. So each of these recipes include no more than five ingredients, supplemented with a handful of staples you should keep on hand: olive oil, vegetable broth, onions, garlic, salt, and pepper.

Each recipe will include a tip with ideas to make the meal tastier, easier, or with a different spin. Although the recipes are meant to stand on their own, never hesitate to supplement your meal. The recipes I am providing are the blueprint to an easy, nutritious, plant-based dish, but I expect you to include other components on the side, like leafy greens, extra vegetables, fruits, grains, legumes, and healthy fats like nuts and seeds.

Remember that we don't count calories on a healthy, unprocessed, whole-food, plant-based diet. The beauty of making plants the center of your plate is that you can eat more without gaining weight. Often you will actually lose weight on a plant-based diet because it consists of vegetables, fruits, grains, legumes, and healthy fats, which are naturally lower in calories and saturated fat. On a plant-based diet, you can fill your plate with as many vegetables as you want because vegetables are so nutrient-dense—low in calories but high in vitamins, minerals, and fiber. Keep in mind, though, that healthy fats like nuts, seeds, and avocados should make up about 10 percent of your daily calories.

Additionally, the back of the book includes two helpful indexes. One is arranged so you can search for recipes by type, and one will help you search by ingredient. These indexes can help you use up leftovers like grains and beans. You can also swap the plant-based protein in many of these recipes, like chickpeas for tofu. Think like a chef and experiment.

I am grateful that you bought a book that celebrates healthy food. We are all connected, and any compassion we show ourselves ripples out to the entire universe, one plant-based meal at a time.

CHAPTER 2

Smoothies
and
Breakfasts

← Blueberry and Grape Brainiac Smoothie, p.23

The Runner's Drink

Serves 1 / Prep time: 10 minutes

GLUTEN-FREE, NUT-FREE, OIL-FREE, SOY-FREE

2 teaspoons chia seeds

1¼ cups water

Juice of 1 lemon or lime

Drizzle of pure
    maple syrup

The Tarahumara people, located in Mexico, are renowned for their long-distance running. They can run up to 200 miles in one session. Before running, they drink a mix called *iskiate*. Iskiate is simply water mixed with ancient Mayan chia seeds. Keep chia seeds in a glass container with a tight-fitting lid and store them in a dark, cool place, like your cupboard.

1. Shake or stir together the chia seeds, water, and citrus juice. Sweeten with a drizzle of maple syrup.

2. Pour over ice and serve.

Substitution Tip: Add ¼ cup of frozen berries for a more tropical drink. Let them sit for 30 minutes to defrost before adding to the drink.

Per serving: Calories: 84; Fat: 4g; Saturated fat: 1g; Carbohydrate: 10g; Fiber: 4g; Sugar: 5g; Protein: 2g; Iron: 1mg; Sodium: 12mg

Blueberry and Grape Brainiac Smoothie

Serves 4 / Prep time: 5 minutes

GLUTEN-FREE, OIL-FREE, SOY-FREE

2 cups blueberries

2 cups seedless red or black grapes

4 cups unsweetened almond milk

2 tablespoons pure maple syrup

4 tablespoons ground flaxseed

1 cup ice cubes

A powerhouse of cognitive ingredients sets this smoothie apart. Scientific studies have shown that polyphenol-rich fruits such as blueberries and grapes can have a dramatic effect on brainpower. So if you are facing a big exam or an important meeting, this smoothie can lead to greater mental alertness. Blueberries are also the queen of antioxidant foods and among the most nutrient-dense. I recommend including blueberries in your diet a few times a week, especially in the winter months when your immune system is weaker.

In a blender or food processor, purée everything together until smooth.

Ingredient Tip: Smoothie recipes are surprisingly simple to make and customize. Just remember this simple formula: fruit + nondairy milk + healthy fat like nuts, avocado, or seeds + ice. Optional add-ins include leafy greens for iron and folate, one frozen banana for extra potassium and vitamin C, a sweetener like maple syrup, and a sugar-free protein powder.

Per serving: Calories: 242; Fat: 11g; Saturated fat: 1g; Carbohydrate: 32g; Fiber: 9g; Sugar: 21g; Protein: 6g; Iron: 4mg; Sodium: 362mg

Overnight Chia Seed Plant-Powered Breakfast

Serves 2 to 3 / Prep time: 5 minutes, plus overnight to set

GLUTEN-FREE, OIL-FREE, SOY-FREE

½ cup chia seeds

2 cups unsweetened almond milk or any unflavored, unsweetened nondairy milk

3 tablespoons pure maple syrup

½ teaspoon vanilla extract

Toppings of your choice: fruits, nuts, seeds, figs, dates, toasted coconut flakes (optional)

This thick and creamy chia seed pudding is naturally sweetened with vanilla and maple syrup. It's also a super-nutritious make-ahead breakfast that takes only a few minutes to prepare. Combine the ingredients the night before, refrigerate, and then eat. Chia seeds fill you up fast and deliver a massive amount of nutrients, including protein. This dish can be refrigerated up to 3 days. Top it with ½ teaspoon finely grated lemon zest for a bright punch.

1. In a container with a lid, thoroughly combine the chia seeds, almond milk, maple syrup, and vanilla. Refrigerate overnight, until the mixture is thick and pudding-like.

2. When you're ready to serve, stir to remove any clumps. Spoon into bowls and customize your breakfast by adding your favorite toppings. I like to include a sweet and crunchy element. Drizzle with a little extra maple syrup, if you'd like.

Ingredient Tip: The basic, easy-to-remember ratio for making chia pudding is ¼ cup chia seeds to 1 cup nondairy milk.

Per serving: Calories: 397; Fat: 21g; Saturated fat: 2g; Carbohydrate: 46g; Fiber: 21g; Sugar: 18g; Protein: 10g; Iron: 5mg; Sodium: 192mg

Baked Oatmeal and Fruit

Serves 4 / Prep time: **5 minutes** / Cook time: **20 minutes**

NUT-FREE, OIL-FREE, SOY-FREE

3 cups quick-
cooking oats

3 cups unflavored,
unsweetened
nondairy milk

¼ cup pure maple syrup

1 tablespoon vanilla
extract

1 to 2 cups blueberries,
raspberries, or both

Healthy baked oatmeal naturally sweetened with maple syrup is a wonderful and delicious way to begin the day. Eating oats is one of the easiest ways to add starch that resists digestion, which can have powerful health benefits, to your diet. These starches can promote a healthy gut, improve blood sugar levels, and increase feelings of fullness to help you eat less. Barley and green plantains are also excellent sources of this starch.

1. Preheat the oven to 375°F.

2. In a large mixing bowl, combine all the ingredients. Pour into a large casserole dish and cover with aluminum foil.

3. Bake for 10 minutes. Uncover and bake for another 5 to 10 minutes, or until all the liquid is visibly gone and the edges start to brown.

4. Let cool 5 minutes before serving. Serve with an extra splash of nondairy milk and a drizzle of maple syrup.

Leftovers: Make a big batch as a quick go-to breakfast for the week. Just reheat in the oven or microwave, or on the stovetop.

Per serving: Calories: 365; Fat: 7g; Saturated fat: 1g; Carbohydrate: 67g; Fiber: 9g; Sugar: 20g; Protein: 9g; Iron: 4mg; Sodium: 141mg

Hemp and Oat Granola

Serves 4 / Prep time: 5 minutes / Cook time: 30 minutes

OIL-FREE, SOY-FREE

2 cups old-fashioned
rolled oats

1½ teaspoons cinnamon

½ cup hemp seeds

⅓ cup slivered almonds

⅓ cup pure maple syrup

This is an Ordinary Vegan community favorite. Homemade granola tastes so much better than store-bought and is much healthier. Serve it with nondairy milk or yogurt, sprinkle over a fruit salad, or use it as a topping for a baked apple. Hemp seeds provide long-lasting energy, so you'll be ready for anything.

1. Preheat the oven to 350°F. Line a large baking sheet with parchment paper.

2. Spread the oats on the lined baking sheet. Sprinkle over the cinnamon and toss. Spread evenly on the baking sheet and toast in the oven for 10 minutes.

3. Add the hemp seeds and toss with the oats. Toast for another 10 minutes. Add the almonds, toss, and toast for another 5 minutes.

4. Remove from oven and drizzle with maple syrup. Toss, spread evenly on the baking sheet, and toast for another 5 minutes.

5. Refrigerate covered for up to 5 days.

Substitution Tip: Substitute sunflower seeds for the hemp seeds or add ½ cup chopped dates or dried fruit.

Per serving: Calories: 434; Fat: 20g; Saturated fat: 2g; Carbohydrate: 49g; Fiber: 6g; Sugar: 16g; Protein: 17g; Iron: 6mg; Sodium: 5mg

Savory Oats with Mushrooms

Serves 4 / Prep time: **10 minutes** / Cook time: **35 minutes**

GLUTEN-FREE, OIL-FREE, NUT-FREE

4 cups low-sodium vegetable broth

⅓ cup low-sodium vegetable broth or 2 teaspoons extra-virgin olive oil for sautéing

3 tablespoons chopped shallots

8 ounces cremini or white button mushrooms, sliced

2 garlic cloves, chopped

1 teaspoon white wine vinegar

2 cups steel-cut oats

4 tablespoons hemp seeds

Swap your typical morning fare for this flavorful, umami-rich breakfast. Often, when we choose a savory meal to begin the day, it includes more fiber, healthy fats, and protein—all of which contribute to blood sugar stability—and the high-fiber oats will help keep you feeling full. Top this dish with a fresh chopped herb such as parsley, or drizzle with a little maple syrup for a savory-sweet flavor.

1. In a large saucepan over medium-high heat, heat the 4 cups of vegetable broth and bring to a simmer.

2. On a separate burner, in another large saucepan over medium-high heat, heat the broth or oil for sautéing. Add the shallots and mushrooms and cook over low heat until the shallots begin to soften but do not brown, 2 to 3 minutes. Add the garlic and cook for 1 minute more. Add the vinegar and stir. Add the steel-cut oats and stir to coat.

3. Add the simmering broth, 1 cup at a time, until each cup is completely absorbed by the oats, stirring frequently. This will take 20 to 30 minutes. By the time the last cup of broth has been absorbed, the oats should be done. Add a little more broth if they need to cook more.

continued →

4. Top each serving with 1 tablespoon of hemp seeds.

Preparation Tip: It can take longer than 30 minutes to cook a bowl of steel-cut oats, but there is a shortcut. Soak the oats overnight in water and then drain, and you will only need to cook them for about 10 minutes.

Per serving: Calories: 269; Fat: 10g; Saturated fat: 0g; Carbohydrate: 32g; Fiber: 5g; Sugar: 1g; Protein: 14g; Iron: 6mg; Sodium: 77mg

Warm Farro with Dried Sweet Cherries and Pistachios

Serves 4 / Prep time: 5 minutes / Cook time: 40 minutes

OIL-FREE, SOY-FREE

2 cups farro

2½ cups water

¼ cup dried
   sweet cherries

¼ cup shelled
   unsalted pistachios

Drizzle of pure
   maple syrup

This colorful grain bowl is a satisfying, delicious, and wonderful way to begin any day. The farro (a type of whole-grain wheat) adds a complex, nutty flavor and is packed with protein. The dried cherries add a vibrant, deep red color and a sweet taste. The pistachios add a creamy texture and rich flavor, and are also an excellent source of protein, fiber, and antioxidants.

1. Place the farro in a fine-mesh colander and rinse with cool water until the water runs clear.

2. In a medium saucepan over high heat, boil the water. Stir in the farro and make sure it is completely submerged in the water. Reduce the heat to a gentle simmer. Cover and cook until the farro is chewy and the water is absorbed. Cooking time can vary from 15 to 30 minutes, and the time can vary even more depending on the type of farro you use, so be sure to read instructions on the package.

3. Check the texture every 5 to 10 minutes. You want it to have a little bite to it. If your farro is done before all the water is absorbed, drain any excess water.

continued →

Warm Farro with Dried Sweet Cherries and Pistachios *continued*

4. Stir in the cherries, then top with the pistachios.

5. Drizzle with maple syrup. Serve warm.

Substitution Tip: For a different flavor profile, try this with raisins and walnuts instead of cherries and pistachios.

Per serving: Calories: 296; Fat: 3g; Saturated fat: 0g; Carbohydrate: 55g; Fiber: 9g; Sugar: 6g; Protein: 10g; Iron: 3mg; Sodium: 3mg

Breakfast in Bed Tofu Spinach Scramble

Serves 4 / Prep time: **5 minutes** / Cook time: **10 minutes**
GLUTEN-FREE, NUT-FREE

1 (14-ounce) package tofu

1 tablespoon nutritional yeast

2 teaspoons ground turmeric

½ **cup low-sodium vegetable broth or 2 teaspoons extra-virgin olive oil for sautéing**

½ onion, chopped

1 tablespoon low-sodium vegetable broth, plus more as needed

3 to 4 cups spinach

Salt

Freshly ground black pepper

Breakfast in bed is one of the ultimate ways to pamper someone. But nothing says you love someone more than serving a breakfast that helps protect them from disease and contributes to their longevity. There are many ways to dress up this dish. Include a squeeze of citrus, some chopped cilantro, or avocado slices, or top with Roasted Tomatillo Salsa (see page 158). Substitute spinach with a peppery green like arugula, add a chopped garlic clove in the sauté, or make burritos by serving the scramble with whole-wheat tortillas.

1. In a large bowl, drain and crumble the tofu. Add the nutritional yeast and turmeric and stir to combine.

2. In a large sauté pan over medium-high heat, heat the broth or oil for sautéing. Add the onion and cook until soft and translucent, 3 to 5 minutes. Add a little more vegetable broth if it's sticking.

continued →

Breakfast in Bed Tofu Spinach Scramble *continued*

3. Add the tofu mixture, spinach, and 1 tablespoon vegetable broth. Cover and cook for another 2 to 4 minutes, or until the spinach has wilted.

4. Season with salt and pepper.

Ingredient Tip: Use any tofu variety, from silken to firm, depending on the texture you prefer.

Per serving: Calories: 103; Fat: 5g; Saturated fat: 1g; Carbohydrate: 6g; Fiber: 3g; Sugar: 1g; Protein: 12g; Iron: 3mg; Sodium: 85mg

Vegan Egg Yolk and Toast

Serves 4 / Prep time: 5 minutes / Cook time: 5 minutes

NUT-FREE, OIL-FREE, SOY-FREE

4 teaspoons cornstarch

2 tablespoons unsweetened almond milk

1 tablespoon nutritional yeast

¼ teaspoon ground turmeric

1 cup water

¼ teaspoon salt

Freshly ground black pepper

4 whole-grain bread slices, toasted

There's no reason to miss a runny egg yolk when you go vegan. Now you can eat your heart out without all the cholesterol! This vegan egg yolk has a silky, creamy texture and beautiful color. It is also completely delicious and fools the mouth and taste buds. If you want that sulfuric egg flavor, add ¼ teaspoon kala namak, a Himalayan black salt. Serve with Portobello Bacon (see page 101).

1. In a medium saucepan over medium heat, whisk together the cornstarch, almond milk, nutritional yeast, turmeric and water. Continue to whisk while it cooks, 3 to 5 minutes or until the vegan yolk sauce thickens.

2. Season with salt and pepper.

3. Serve the yolk sauce in small bowls, with the toast on the side for dipping.

Serving Suggestion: For the full eggs-perience, cut some tofu into thin slices and sauté in vegan butter. Use a shot glass to make a round hole in the middle of each one. Spoon the vegan egg yolk into each hole.

Per serving: Calories: 104; Fat: 1g; Saturated fat: 0g; Carbohydrate: 17g; Fiber: 3g; Sugar: 1g; Protein: 6g; Iron: 1mg; Sodium: 304mg

Kimchi and Kale Breakfast Scramble

Serves 4 / Prep time: **10 minutes** / Cook time: **10 minutes**

GLUTEN-FREE, NUT-FREE

⅓ cup low-sodium
  vegetable broth
  or 2 teaspoons
  extra-virgin olive oil
  for sautéing

3 tablespoons chopped
  shallots

2 garlic cloves, chopped

1 (14-ounce) package
  firm tofu, drained

2½ tablespoons gluten-
  free soy sauce
  or tamari

½ cup kale, ribs
  removed, cut
  into ribbons

1 cup vegan kimchi,
  chopped

Salt

**Freshly ground
  black pepper**

This scramble is a quick, protein-packed, plant-based breakfast. What makes this scramble special is the probiotic kimchi. Probiotics are live microorganisms that promote a healthy digestive tract and immune system. The main flavor notes of kimchi include sour, spicy, and umami. Because kimchi is a fermented dish, it has a prominent sour flavor that may take some getting used to. Although it's cabbage-based, not all kimchi is vegan; it can contain fish sauce or some kind of fermented fish. Make sure the label says "vegan."

1. In a large skillet over medium-high heat, heat the broth or oil for sautéing. Add the shallots and cook until they begin to soften but do not brown, 2 to 3 minutes. Add the garlic and cook for 1 minute more.

2. Press the water out of the tofu with a clean dishcloth. Add the tofu, crumbling it between your fingers. Add the soy sauce. Cook for 2 minutes.

3. Add the kale ribbons and cook until they become soft and wilted, about 3 minutes.

4. Add the kimchi, and cook until it's warmed through, about 1 minute. (Live probiotic cultures are destroyed at 115°F, so you should add the kimchi at the end of cooking to preserve the health benefits.)

5. Season with salt and pepper.

Serving Suggestion: Add 2 teaspoons grated ginger to the sauté. Squeeze some fresh lime juice on top and serve with whole-wheat tortillas.

Per serving: Calories: 92; Fat: 4g; Saturated fat: 1g; Carbohydrate: 6g; Fiber: 1g; Sugar: 1g; Protein: 10g; Iron: 2mg; Sodium: 710mg

CHAPTER 3

Salads

← Kale, Blood Orange, and Walnut Salad, p.44

Pineapple, Cucumber, and Mint Salad

Serves 4 / Prep time: 10 minutes

GLUTEN-FREE, NUT-FREE, OIL-FREE, SOY-FREE

3 cups chopped fresh pineapple

3 cups fresh cucumber, peeled, seeded, and sliced

3 scallions, thinly sliced

¼ cup chopped fresh mint

¼ cup fresh lime juice

Pineapple is rich in vitamin C and packed with disease-fighting antioxidants. It also delivers fiber, which can help control your blood sugar level and keep you feeling full. This bright, refreshing salad also makes a great topping for grilled tofu.

In a large bowl, combine all the ingredients and gently toss.

Substitution Tip: Lime juice too tart? Combine a little maple syrup with the fresh juice or a small amount of olive oil if you are not oil-free. Add some thinly sliced Fresno chile to bring some heat. Or for a different flavor, replace the pineapple with papaya, guava, or mango.

Storage Tip: At room temperature, a ripe pineapple will stay fresh for around 3 days. Whole pineapples shouldn't be stored in the refrigerator, but once the flesh has been peeled and chopped, it's fine to chill in an airtight container.

Per serving: Calories: 82; Fat: 0g; Saturated fat: 0g; Carbohydrate: 21g; Fiber: 3g; Sugar: 14g; Protein: 2g; Iron: 1mg; Sodium: 7mg

Bright, Beautiful Slaw

Serves 4 / Prep time: 15 minutes

GLUTEN-FREE, NUT-FREE, OIL-FREE, SOY-FREE

Juice and zest of 2 limes

¼ cup pure maple syrup

Salt

**Freshly ground
black pepper**

4 to 5 cups red cabbage,
finely shredded

2 mangos or papayas,
cut into small chunks

2 cups roughly chopped
mint leaves

This crisp, fresh salad owes its crunch to red cabbage and its sweet juicy flavor to the tropical fruit. The refreshing, cool zing comes courtesy of mint. Red cabbage has a wealth of phytochemicals, antioxidants, nutrients, vitamins, and minerals. Its beneficial compounds are almost too numerous to list, and its antioxidants are powerful, too.

1. In a small bowl, whisk together the lime juice and maple syrup. Season with salt and pepper. Set aside.

2. In a medium bowl, add the red cabbage, mango, mint, and lime zest.

3. Add the dressing a little at a time and toss together. Taste and season again with salt and pepper.

Ingredient Tip: Tropical fruits like mangos and papayas are best to keep out of the refrigerator because they are sensitive to cold temperatures. They will continue to ripen at room temperature, becoming sweeter over a few days. To speed up ripening, place in a paper bag at room temperature until the fruit is ripe.

Per serving: Calories: 177; Fat: 1g; Saturated fat: 0g; Carbohydrate: 44g; Fiber: 5g; Sugar: 38g; Protein: 3g; Iron: 1mg; Sodium: 58mg

Fennel and Mint Salad

Serves 4 / Prep time: 10 minutes

GLUTEN-FREE, NUT-FREE, OIL-FREE, SOY-FREE

Juice and zest of
  2 lemons

4 teaspoons pure
  maple syrup

Salt

**Freshly ground
  black pepper**

4 cups chopped baby
  romaine lettuce

2 large fennel bulbs, cut
  into thin slices, plus
  the fronds

½ cup roughly torn fresh
  mint leaves

This salad unites the beautiful anise flavor of fennel with the sweet and cool taste of mint: a lovely, simple combination that proves a few ingredients can bring a powerhouse of flavor. If you want to make this an entrée, add a cup of cooked beans or a whole grain for additional protein.

1. In a small bowl, whisk together the lemon juice and maple syrup. Season with salt and pepper and set aside.

2. In a large bowl, toss the romaine lettuce, lemon zest, fennel slices, and mint.

3. Strip the fronds from the fennel stalks and toss them into the salad.

4. Lightly dress with the lemon dressing. Season with salt and pepper.

Serving Suggestion: Sometimes I top this salad with ¼ cup chopped unsalted pistachios or a sliced tart apple.

Per serving: Calories: 66; Fat: 1g; Saturated fat: 0g; Carbohydrate: 15g; Fiber: 5g; Sugar: 5g; Protein: 2g; Iron: 2mg; Sodium: 108mg

Cannellini Bean Salad with Avocado and Tomato

Serves 3 to 4 / Prep time: 10 minutes

GLUTEN-FREE, NUT-FREE, OIL-FREE, SOY-FREE

3 to 5 tablespoons fresh lemon juice, divided

2 avocados, roughly mashed

2 (15.5-ounce) cans cannellini beans, drained and rinsed

¾ cup chopped red onion

½ cup chopped fresh basil

4 garlic cloves, minced

Salt

Freshly ground black pepper

3 tomatoes, sliced

Who doesn't love an easy bean salad? This Italian-inspired salad couldn't be simpler or pack more flavor. If you have never tried them, cannellini beans are broad white beans popular in Italian cuisine for their velvety flavor. Canned are convenient, but of course you can also cook them fresh if you have the time. Drizzle a teaspoon of olive oil on top of the salad, if you include it in your diet.

1. In a medium bowl, add 2 tablespoons of lemon juice to the avocado and roughly mash.

2. In a large bowl, combine the beans, onion, basil, garlic, and 1½ tablespoons of the lemon juice. Season with salt and pepper. Add more lemon juice if needed.

3. Spread the avocado mixture on a large serving plate. Layer the tomato slices over the avocado.

4. Layer the bean mixture over the top. Season with salt and pepper.

continued →

Cannellini Bean Salad with Avocado and Tomato *continued*

Ingredient Tip: One cup of cannellini beans contains only 225 calories, 15 grams of protein, and 0.9 grams of fat. They are also a wonderful source of fiber, folate, and iron, so I recommend putting this salad into regular rotation.

Per serving: Calories: 348; Fat: 14g; Saturated fat: 2g; Carbohydrate: 45g; Fiber: 18g; Sugar: 5g; Protein: 15g; Iron: 5mg; Sodium: 58mg

Mock Tuna Salad

Serves 4 / Prep time: 10 minutes

GLUTEN-FREE, NUT-FREE

4 cups cooked
  chickpeas,
  lightly mashed

**4 to 5 tablespoons
  chopped red onion**

1½ cups chopped
  celery stalks

¼ cup plus
  2 tablespoons
  chopped pickles

¼ cup vegan
  mayonnaise or
  Tofu Mayonnaise
  (page 150)

Salt

**Freshly ground
  black pepper**

8 large romaine or
  iceberg lettuce leaves

This recipe is a perfect example of how it's not the protein we miss in a vegan diet, but the flavors. Chickpeas do a great job standing in for tuna in this recipe. This vegan take on a classic salad is also extremely flavorful and filling. You can use store-bought vegan mayonnaise or create your own oil-free Tofu Mayonnaise (see page 150). Add ¼ cup of unsalted roasted sunflower seeds for added crunch and nutrition.

1. In a large bowl, combine the chickpeas, onion, celery, pickles, and mayonnaise and mix well. Add more mayonnaise if needed.

2. Season with salt and pepper. Serve over the lettuce leaves.

Leftovers: Any leftover salad is great in sandwiches or wraps.

Per serving: Calories: 320; Fat: 8g; Saturated fat: 1g; Carbohydrate: 49g; Fiber: 14g; Sugar: 9g; Protein: 15g; Iron: 5mg; Sodium: 368mg

Kale, Blood Orange, and Walnut Salad

Serves 4 / Prep time: 10 minutes / Cook time: 10 minutes

GLUTEN-FREE, OIL-FREE, SOY-FREE

3 to 4 blood oranges

1 tablespoon pure
  maple syrup

2 tablespoons white
  wine vinegar

2 garlic cloves, chopped

¼ teaspoon salt

**Freshly ground
  black pepper**

¼ cup chopped walnuts

4 cups kale, ribs
  removed, cut
  into ribbons

This bright, citrusy, flavorful winter salad is loaded with vitamin C and a burst of beautiful color. Vitamin C is an essential vitamin, meaning it can't be produced by the body, and the more you eat, the more it boosts the immune system. Anthocyanins, pigment that's common in flowers but not in fruit, are what make blood oranges deep red. If you can't find them, substitute any variety of orange or grapefruit.

1. Juice 2 to 3 blood oranges, until you have ⅓ cup juice. Peel and section the remaining oranges.

2. Combine ⅓ cup blood orange juice, maple syrup, vinegar, garlic, salt, and ground black pepper in a food processor. Process until smooth. Taste and add a little water if needed.

3. Heat the oven to 350°F.

4. Spread the walnuts in a single layer on a baking sheet. Roast for 5 to 10 minutes, tossing the nuts occasionally to ensure even cooking. They are done when they appear a shade darker and smell toasty. Keep a close eye so they don't burn.

5. Place the kale in a large bowl. Add a small amount of the dressing and massage the dressing into the kale for about 2 minutes to soften it, being careful not to overdress.

6. Add the remaining blood orange segments and the toasted walnuts, and drizzle with a little more dressing, if needed.

Serving Suggestion: Add dried tart cherries or a leftover wheat grain like farro to amp up the protein. For a thicker dressing, add 1 tablespoon olive oil as you are processing it.

Per serving: Calories: 223; Fat: 7g; Saturated fat: 1g; Carbohydrate: 39g; Fiber: 7g; Sugar: 25g; Protein: 6g; Iron: 2mg; Sodium: 178mg

Rich and Creamy Caesar Salad

Serves 4 / Prep time: **10 minutes** / Cook time: **10 minutes**

NUT-FREE, SOY-FREE

3 whole-wheat bread slices, cut into small cubes

1 teaspoon extra-virgin olive oil

1 cup chopped avocado

3 tablespoons fresh lemon juice

2 garlic cloves, chopped

½ to 1 cup water

Salt

Freshly ground black pepper

1 romaine lettuce head

½ cup small capers, drained

This vegan Caesar salad has all the tanginess and creaminess you'd expect from a traditional Caesar salad, without the eggs and anchovies. I often sprinkle this salad with ¼ cup ground pine nuts, which adds a salty Parmesan-like flavor and extra protein. To save time, you can wash and spin dry the lettuce in a salad spinner ahead of time. Store the spun lettuce in a covered glass bowl with a paper towel on top.

1. Preheat the oven to 450°F.

2. On a large baking sheet, toss the bread cubes with the oil. (If you are oil-free, omit the oil.) Spread them in a single layer and bake until brown and crisp. Watch carefully, because this should only take 5 to 10 minutes.

3. In a blender, blend the avocado, garlic, lemon juice, and some of the water. Keep adding a little water at a time until you have the right consistency. Season with salt and pepper.

4. Wash and dry the romaine leaves. Cut into bite-size pieces and place in salad bowl. Toss with the capers, croutons, and a small amount of dressing, adding more as needed (you might not need all the dressing).

Ingredient Tip: Keep unripe avocados at room temperature. To speed up the ripening process, put them in a paper bag on your counter. When the skin is black or dark purple and yields to gentle pressure, it's ready to eat or refrigerate.

Per serving: Calories: 156; Fat: 9g; Saturated fat: 2g; Carbohydrate: 16g; Fiber: 5g; Sugar: 3g; Protein: 4g; Iron: 3mg; Sodium: 657mg

Curried Potato Salad

Serves 4 / Prep time: 10 minutes / Cook time: 10 minutes

GLUTEN-FREE, NUT-FREE, OIL-FREE

3 medium baking
   potatoes, peeled and
   cut into ½-inch cubes

**½ cup finely
   chopped onion**

½ (14-ounce) package
   soft tofu

½ tablespoon pure
   maple syrup

½ teaspoon Dijon
   mustard

Salt

**Freshly ground
   black pepper**

1 tablespoon
   curry powder

Curried potato salad blends the classic picnic side dish with savory and earthy Indian flavors. Many people forget the health benefits of the humble potato, because in the past few years white potatoes have been bashed and placed on the dreaded "white foods" list. But I am here to tell you that besides being cost-effective, white potatoes are one of the healthiest foods you can eat. Potatoes contain resistant starch, a particular kind of starch that isn't broken down by the small intestine. As the fibers ferment, they act as a prebiotic and feed the good bacteria in your gut.

1. Bring a medium pot of water to a boil and add the potatoes. Cook for about 10 minutes, until they are soft but still have a bite. Do not overcook. Drain and place in a medium bowl with the onion to cool.

2. Add the tofu, maple syrup, and mustard to a food processor or blender and process until smooth. If needed, add a few teaspoons of water for the right consistency. Season with salt and pepper.

3. Add ½ cup of the tofu mixture and the curry powder to the bowl of potatoes and combine well. Taste and add a little more salt, pepper, and curry powder if needed.

Substitution Tip: To make this recipe soy-free, replace the tofu with ¼ cup store-bought vegan mayonnaise. For different flavors, you can also substitute sweet potatoes for the white potatoes and replace the onion with ¼ cup or more of chopped scallions.

Per serving: Calories: 159; Fat: 2g; Saturated fat: 0g; Carbohydrate: 30g; Fiber: 5g; Sugar: 4g; Protein: 6g; Iron: 2mg; Sodium: 61mg

Spinach and Sweet Potato Salad with Tahini Dressing

Serves 4 / Prep time: **10 minutes** / Cook time: **25 minutes**

GLUTEN-FREE, NUT-FREE, SOY-FREE

4 large sweet potatoes, unpeeled, cut into ½-inch cubes

3 tablespoons low-sodium vegetable broth or 2 teaspoons extra-virgin olive oil for cooking

½ cup tahini

¼ cup fresh lemon juice (from 3 to 4 lemons)

2 to 3 garlic cloves, minced

¼ cup water

8 cups spinach

¼ cup shelled toasted pumpkin seeds

Salt

Freshly ground black pepper

Roasting the sweet potatoes brings out tender, caramelized flavors, and the creamy, rich tahini and lemon juice brighten up any dish. I call the sweet potato the fountain of youth. The people of Okinawa have a life expectancy among the highest in the world, and more than 25 percent of their diet consists of sweet potatoes.

1. Preheat the oven to 400°F.

2. In a large glass baking dish or on a parchment paper–lined baking sheet, arrange the sweet potatoes in a single layer. Sprinkle the vegetable broth or oil over them.

3. Roast for 20 to 25 minutes, stirring once halfway through, until the potatoes are crisp on the outside and tender on the inside. Remove from the oven and cool slightly.

4. Meanwhile, in a medium bowl, whisk together the tahini, lemon juice, and garlic. Add the water to thin it out, if necessary.

5. In a large salad bowl, toss the spinach with a small amount of dressing. Continue adding dressing until you get the desired amount. Top with the cooked sweet potatoes and pumpkin seeds. Season with salt and pepper.

Preparation Tip: Roasting pumpkin seeds brings out nutty and sweet flavors. Preheat the oven to 325°F. Spread the pumpkin seeds on a medium baking sheet. Sprinkle lightly with salt. Bake 25 to 35 minutes, stirring occasionally, until lightly toasted. Keep a watchful eye so they don't burn.

Per serving: Calories: 330; Fat: 18g; Saturated fat: 3g; Carbohydrate: 36g; Fiber: 8g; Sugar: 6g; Protein: 10g; Iron: 6mg; Sodium: 218mg

Edamame and Quinoa Salad

Serves 4 / Prep time: **10 minutes** / Cook time: **20 minutes**

GLUTEN-FREE, NUT-FREE, OIL-FREE

2 cups water

1 cup quinoa, rinsed

3 tablespoons fresh lime juice

3 tablespoons white wine champagne vinegar

1½ tablespoons pure maple syrup

2 garlic cloves, finely chopped

Salt

Freshly ground black pepper

4 tablespoons, finely chopped white or red onion

1 cup frozen cooked edamame, defrosted

This is one of my favorite go-to salads. Not only is it refreshing and zesty, it is also a power duo of complete proteins from the quinoa and edamame—immature soybeans. Complete proteins contain all the essential amino acids our bodies can't produce. Be sure to buy shelled edamame, so you don't have to pop them all out of their pods. Substitute your favorite whole grain for the quinoa—which is actually a seed!

1. In a medium saucepan, bring the water to a boil. Add the quinoa, cover, and lower the heat to a simmer. Cook until all the water is absorbed, keeping a close eye so it doesn't stick, 13 to 18 minutes. Leave covered and set aside.

2. In a small bowl, whisk together the lime juice, vinegar, maple syrup, and garlic. Season with salt and pepper. Set aside.

3. In a large serving bowl, combine the quinoa with the chopped onion and edamame. Add the dressing a little at a time. Mix gently.

4. Taste and adjust the seasoning. Add more dressing if needed, but avoid overdressing.

Serving Suggestion: Make this salad a power trio of protein and add 1 (15.5-ounce) can of black beans that have been drained and rinsed. Serve with a side of leafy greens.

Per serving: Calories: 215; Fat: 4g; Saturated fat: 0g; Carbohydrate: 37g; Fiber: 5g; Sugar: 5g; Protein: 10g; Iron: 3mg; Sodium: 48mg

CHAPTER 4

Soups
and Chili

← Red Bell Pepper Soup with Fresh Basil, p.58

Curried Butternut Squash Soup

Serves 4 / Prep time: 15 minutes / Cook time: 40 minutes
GLUTEN-FREE, NUT-FREE, SOY-FREE

⅓ cup low-sodium
vegetable broth
or 2 teaspoons
extra-virgin olive oil
for sautéing

1 cup chopped onion

3 garlic cloves, chopped

3 tablespoons minced
fresh ginger

2½ pounds butternut
squash, peeled,
seeded, and cut
into chunks

2 to 3 cups low-sodium
vegetable broth,
divided

1 teaspoon curry powder

1 (13.5-ounce) can light
coconut milk

2 tablespoons pure
maple syrup

¼ teaspoon salt

Freshly ground
black pepper

This soup is really creamy yet light. The infusion of curry gives it a savory and sweet flavor. Butternut squash is low in calories but high in nutrients, including vitamins A and C, magnesium, and potassium. When choosing a butternut squash, make sure the skin has a matte look. If it's shiny, it's not ripe yet.

1. In a large saucepan over medium-high heat, heat the broth or oil for sautéing. Add the onion and cook until soft and translucent, 3 to 5 minutes.

2. Add the garlic and ginger and continue to stir and sauté for another minute or two.

3. Add the squash, 2 cups of the vegetable broth, and the curry powder. Bring to a boil, then lower to a simmer. Stir and cook for 15 minutes. Add the coconut milk and maple syrup and cook for another 10 minutes, or until the squash is soft.

4. Remove from the heat and cool. Purée in a food processor or blender to achieve a creamy texture. Add more vegetable broth if the soup is too thick.

5. Reheat the soup for 10 minutes more, and season with salt and pepper.

Serving Suggestion: Top this soup with a dollop of Cashew Sour Cream (see page 151). You can also substitute pumpkin or your favorite winter squash for the butternut.

Per serving: Calories: 254; Fat: 5g; Saturated fat: 4g; Carbohydrate: 53g; Fiber: 7g; Sugar: 17g; Protein: 4g; Iron: 3mg; Sodium: 297mg

Red Bell Pepper Soup with Fresh Basil

Serves 4 / Prep time: 30 minutes / Cook time: 35 minutes

GLUTEN-FREE, NUT-FREE, SOY-FREE

½ cup shelled pumpkin seeds

¼ teaspoon salt, plus a pinch, divided

⅓ cup low-sodium vegetable broth or 2 teaspoons extra-virgin olive oil for sautéing

1 cup chopped onion

4 large red bell peppers, seeded and diced

2 garlic cloves, chopped

2 (14-ounce) cans diced tomatoes

Pinch saffron or ½ teaspoon ground turmeric

3 cups low-sodium vegetable broth

Freshly ground black pepper

3 tablespoons thinly sliced fresh basil

This rich, creamy, vibrant soup has a satisfying long-simmering flavor accented by the sweet and floral scent of saffron. The red bell peppers are an excellent source of healthy vitamins because they contain a compound called capsaicin. The hotter the pepper, the more capsaicin it contains. Studies have found that capsaicin can help with weight loss by speeding up metabolism.

1. Preheat the oven to 375°F.

2. On a large parchment paper–lined baking sheet, spread the pumpkin seeds in a single layer. Sprinkle with a pinch salt. Bake 20 to 30 minutes, stopping to shake the pan every 5 minutes, until the seeds are golden brown. Remove from the oven and set aside.

3. In a large saucepan over medium heat, heat the broth or oil for sautéing. Add the onion and red bell peppers and sauté for 4 to 5 minutes, or until the vegetables begin to soften. Add the garlic and cook for another minute. Stir in the tomatoes, cover, and simmer for another 2 to 3 minutes or until the tomatoes are soft. Stir in the saffron, the remaining ¼ teaspoon salt, and 3 cups vegetable broth. Simmer, partially covered, for 30 minutes. Remove from the heat and let cool.

4. Transfer to a blender or food processor and process until smooth. Do not overprocess or the soup will discolor. Add a little more vegetable broth if soup is too thick.

5. Strain the soup through a fine-mesh sieve and return it to the saucepan to heat through. Season with black pepper and taste for salt.

6. Serve in soup bowls and garnish with basil. Top with a handful of toasted pumpkin seeds.

Ingredient Tip: Red bell peppers should be firm when you buy them. Store them unwashed in a paper bag in the vegetable drawer. It's important to keep them dry, as moisture will cause them to rot.

Per serving: Calories: 139; Fat: 4g; Saturated fat: 1g; Carbohydrate: 22g; Fiber: 5g; Sugar: 13g; Protein: 6g; Iron: 2mg; Sodium: 288mg

Chickpea Soup with Cabbage, Tomatoes, and Basil

Serves 4 / Prep time: **15 minutes** / Cook time: **25 minutes**

GLUTEN-FREE, NUT-FREE, SOY-FREE

⅓ **cup low-sodium vegetable broth or 2 teaspoons extra-virgin olive oil for sautéing**

1 cup chopped onion

1 tablespoon dried basil

½ teaspoon salt

Freshly ground black pepper

4 garlic cloves, chopped

3 cups diced tomatoes, fresh or canned

1 green cabbage head, chopped into bite-size pieces

2 (15.5-ounce) cans chickpeas, drained and rinsed

3 to 4 cups low-sodium vegetable broth

The simple combination of cabbage, chickpeas, basil, and tomatoes tastes so good, you'll want to make this recipe over and over again. Cruciferous vegetables like cabbage are low-calorie and rich in folate, fiber, and vitamins C, E, and K. Chickpeas, also known as garbanzo beans, offer a great vegan source of protein. Half a cup of cooked chickpeas contains about 8 grams of protein.

1. In a large saucepan over medium-high heat, heat the broth or oil for sautéing. Add the onion, basil, and salt, and season with pepper. Sauté until the onion is soft and translucent, 3 to 5 minutes. Add the garlic and sauté for another minute.

2. Add the diced tomatoes, cabbage, and chickpeas. Pour in the 3 cups vegetable broth. Bring to a boil, then simmer for 15 to 20 minutes, or until the cabbage is cooked. Add more vegetable broth if needed; taste and season with salt and pepper if needed.

Per serving: Calories: 302; Fat: 4g; Saturated fat: 0g; Carbohydrate: 55g; Fiber: 16g; Sugar: 17g; Protein: 15g; Iron: 5mg; Sodium: 402mg

Easy Corn Chowder

Serves 4 / Prep time: **15 minutes** / Cook time: **20 minutes**

GLUTEN-FREE, NUT-FREE, SOY-FREE

3 ears fresh sweet corn, or 2¼ cups frozen sweet corn kernels

⅓ cup low-sodium vegetable broth or 2 teaspoons extra-virgin olive oil for sautéing

¼ teaspoon salt

Freshly ground black pepper

1 cup onion, diced

2 small red bell peppers, seeded and diced

3 to 4 cups low-sodium vegetable broth

2 cups yellow or red potatoes, skin on, cut into ½-inch cubes

3 tablespoons chopped fresh dill, plus extra for garnish

½ cup unsweetened almond milk

This easy corn chowder highlights the sweet taste of summer corn any time of the year. Bonus nutrients include vitamin A, vitamin C, iron, and calcium. Keep corn on the cob fresh by wrapping it tightly in a bag and storing it in the refrigerator. For convenience, you can't beat frozen corn. It is frozen when sweet corn is at its peak, takes less time to prepare, and can often be less expensive.

1. Use a sharp knife to slice down along the cob and remove the kernels.

2. In a large saucepan over medium-high heat, heat the broth or oil for sautéing. Season with salt and pepper. Add the onion and red bell peppers. Sauté for 4 to 5 minutes or until the vegetables are soft.

3. Add the 3 cups vegetable broth, then add the potatoes and dill. Season with salt and pepper. Bring to a gentle boil, reduce the heat, and simmer for about 10 minutes. You may need a little extra vegetable broth to cover the potatoes.

4. Add the corn and almond milk and simmer, uncovered, for another 7 minutes or until the potatoes and corn are cooked. Taste and adjust the seasonings.

5. Garnish with more fresh dill.

continued →

Easy Corn Chowder *continued*

Preparation Tip: For the easiest and safest way to remove kernels from corn on the cob, place a small bowl upside down inside a large bowl. Then stand the large end of the corn on top of the smaller bowl. Use a sharp knife to slice down along the cob. The kernels will collect in the bottom of the bigger bowl.

Per serving: Calories: 213; Fat: 2g; Saturated fat: 0g; Carbohydrate: 45g; Fiber: 6g; Sugar: 9g; Protein: 8g; Iron: 3mg; Sodium: 641mg

Black-Eyed Pea Soup with Greens

Serves 4 / Prep time: **10 minutes** / Cook time: **20 minutes**

GLUTEN-FREE, NUT-FREE, SOY-FREE

⅓ **cup low-sodium vegetable broth or 2 teaspoons extra-virgin olive oil for sautéing**

1¼ **cups chopped onion**

1 **teaspoon ground fennel seeds**

4 **garlic cloves, chopped**

3 **(15.5-ounce) cans black-eyed peas, drained and rinsed**

6 **tablespoons nutritional yeast**

3 **to 4 cups low-sodium vegetable broth**

Salt

Freshly ground black pepper

1 **large bunch (about 12 ounces) spinach**

1 **lemon, cut into 4 wedges**

Fennel seeds and nutritional yeast make this soup burst with flavor. The black-eyed peas have an earthier flavor than most beans, making this soup extra satisfying, and the flavonoids in beans can help reduce heart disease and cancer risk. Nutritional yeast is a yellow flaky seasoning with a savory, cheesy, salty flavor. Most regular grocery stores in North America carry it these days.

1. In large saucepan over medium-high heat, heat the broth or oil for sautéing. Add the onion and fennel seeds. Cook until the onion is soft and translucent, 3 to 5 minutes. Add the garlic. Cook for another 2 minutes, adding more vegetable broth if needed.

2. Add the black-eyed peas, nutritional yeast, and 3 cups vegetable broth. Lightly season with salt and pepper. Stir and bring to a light boil, lower the heat, and cook for another 15 minutes, adding more vegetable broth if needed. Add the spinach and cook for another 3 minutes.

3. Season with salt and pepper. Ladle into bowls and serve with lemon wedges on the side.

continued →

Black-Eyed Pea Soup with Greens *continued*

Tool Tip: Buy an inexpensive spice grinder, or a coffee grinder that you use only for spices. For maximum flavor, I recommend starting with whole spices like fennel seeds and grinding them as you need them. Grinding the seeds releases the oils, for much more flavor—but that flavor dissipates quickly if the ground spices sit around.

Per serving: Calories: 389; Fat: 5g; Saturated fat: 0g; Carbohydrate: 63g; Fiber: 20g; Sugar: 2g; Protein: 33g; Iron: 9mg; Sodium: 254mg

Pearl Barley and Kidney Bean Miso Soup

Serves 4 / Prep time: **10 minutes** / Cook time: **1 hour**

NUT-FREE

2 cups uncooked
  pearl barley

5 cups water

⅓ **cup low-sodium
  vegetable broth
  or 2 teaspoons
  extra-virgin olive oil
  for sautéing**

1¼ cups chopped onion

2 garlic cloves, chopped

**3 to 4 cups low-sodium
  vegetable broth**

4 carrots, chopped

2 cups cooked red
  beans, drained
  and rinsed

4 tablespoons white
  miso paste

**Freshly ground
  black pepper**

Adding miso to this soup creates a delicious, lush, umami flavor. The nutty, slightly chewy pearl barley adds a robust and flavorful taste, making this soup a satisfying, filling meal you'll want to make often.

1. Put the barley and water in a large stockpot and bring to a boil. Reduce the heat to a simmer and cook, covered, until the barley is tender and most of the liquid has been absorbed, 30 to 40 minutes. Let stand for 5 minutes. You want the barley to still have a little bite.

2. In a large saucepan over medium-high heat, heat the broth or oil for sautéing. Add the onion and cook until soft and translucent, 3 to 4 minutes. Add the garlic and cook for 1 minute more.

3. Add 3 cups vegetable broth to the saucepan. Bring to a boil. Add the carrots and simmer for 15 minutes. Add the cooked barley and beans and simmer for another 10 minutes, adding more vegetable broth if needed.

4. Remove from the heat and stir in the miso paste. Taste and season with pepper.

continued →

Pearl Barley and Kidney Bean Miso Soup *continued*

Ingredient Tip: Miso is a traditional Japanese seasoning made from fermented soybeans, salt, rice, barley, and other ingredients. The darker the color, the saltier and stronger the flavor.

Per serving: Calories: 556; Fat: 3g; Saturated fat: 0g; Carbohydrate: 112g; Fiber: 25g; Sugar: 6g; Protein: 23g; Iron: 6mg; Sodium: 917mg

Roasted Rosemary Beet Soup with Toasted Sunflower Seeds

Serves 4 / Prep time: **20 minutes** / Cook time: **1 hour 10 minutes**

NUT-FREE, GLUTEN-FREE, SOY-FREE

5 to 6 medium beets

3 tablespoons finely chopped rosemary, plus 5 or 6 small sprigs

½ cup sunflower seeds

⅓ **cup low-sodium vegetable broth or 2 teaspoons extra-virgin olive oil for sautéing**

4 to 5 tablespoons minced shallots

2 to 2½ cups vegetable broth

½ **teaspoon salt**

Fresh ground black pepper

Fresh beets make a healthy, vibrant, and gorgeous soup that is perfect any time of year. Beets come in a rainbow of colors, so choose any color you'd like for this soup. And the beets pair perfectly with the most aromatic and pungent of all herbs, rosemary. Sunflower seeds add a nice crunch and a nutty flavor. Top with a dollop of Cashew Sour Cream (see page 151) and some fresh chopped chives.

1. Preheat the oven to 400°F.

2. Wash the beets thoroughly and place each beet with a sprig of rosemary on an individual sheet of aluminum foil. Fold each one into a loose packet and transfer to a large baking sheet. Roast the beets for 50 minutes or until they are easily pierced with a knife. Set aside to cool. When they have cooled enough to handle them, remove the skin and cube the beets. Discard the rosemary sprigs.

3. Meanwhile, heat the sunflower seeds in a heavy dry skillet over medium heat for 1 to 2 minutes, or until light brown and aromatic. Shake the skillet frequently for even browning. Immediately remove from pan and set aside.

continued →

4. In a large saucepan over medium heat, heat
the broth or oil for sautéing. Add the shallots
and chopped rosemary and sauté until soft
and translucent, 3 to 4 minutes. Stir in the
cooked beets, 1½ cups vegetable broth, salt, and
pepper. Bring to a boil, reduce the heat, and
simmer for 15 minutes. Remove from heat and
let cool.

5. Transfer the soup to a blender and purée in
batches. Add more vegetable broth until you
reach the desired consistency. Return the soup
to the saucepan to reheat.

6. To serve, sprinkle 2 tablespoons of roasted
sunflower seeds over each bowl.

Ingredient Tip: To store beets, trim the leaves
2 inches from the root bulb. Do not trim the taproot. Store
the root bulbs in bags in the refrigerator crisper drawer for
7 to 10 days.

Per serving: Calories: 134; Fat: 4g; Saturated fat: 1g;
Carbohydrate: 19g; Fiber: 4g; Sugar: 13g; Protein: 7g; Iron: 2mg;
Sodium: 566mg

Split Pea and Green Pea Soup with Fresh Mint

Serves 4 / Prep time: 10 minutes / Cook time: 45 minutes

GLUTEN-FREE, NUT-FREE, SOY-FREE

⅓ cup low-sodium
vegetable broth
or 2 teaspoons
extra-virgin olive oil
for sautéing

2 leeks, chopped
(about 2 cups)

1½ cups dried yellow or
green split peas, rinsed

**4 to 5 cups low-sodium
vegetable broth**

1½ cups frozen
green peas

¼ cup chopped
fresh mint

¼ cup chopped fresh
parsley

¼ teaspoon salt

**Freshly ground
black pepper**

The one-two punch of split peas and green peas in this healthy soup is perfection. Fresh leeks should be stored unwashed and untrimmed in the refrigerator, where they'll keep for 1 to 2 weeks. Make sure to wash them carefully before using, to remove grit and dirt between layers.

1. In a large nonstick pot over medium-high heat, heat the broth or oil for sautéing. Add the leeks. Sauté until the leeks wilt, 3 to 4 minutes. Add a little more veggie broth, if needed.

2. Add the split peas and stir. Add 4 cups vegetable broth and bring to a boil. Reduce the heat to medium-low. Simmer until split peas are tender, about 30 minutes or more, adding more vegetable broth if needed.

3. Add the frozen peas and another cup of broth, if needed. Bring to a boil and simmer for another 5 minutes. Remove from the heat and stir in the chopped mint and parsley.

4. Transfer about half the soup to a blender. Purée until smooth. Return to the saucepan. With the rest of the soup.

5. Taste and season with salt and pepper.

Per serving: Calories: 342; Fat: 1g; Saturated fat: 0g; Carbohydrate: 62g; Fiber: 23g; Sugar: 12g; Protein: 22g; Iron: 6mg; Sodium: 314mg

Barb's Soup Dumplings

Serves 4 to 6 / Prep time: **10 minutes** / Cook time: **10 minutes**

GLUTEN-FREE, NUT-FREE, OIL-FREE, SOY-FREE

1 cup chickpea flour or flour of your choice

½ cup cornmeal

2 teaspoons baking powder

½ **teaspoon salt**

2 to 3 tablespoons **low-sodium vegetable broth or vegan butter**

⅔ cup unflavored, unsweetened nondairy milk

2 tablespoons minced fresh parsley

Freshly ground black pepper

Many years ago, my girlfriend Barb sent me a recipe for soup dumplings. I have been making them ever since. They are a fun and satisfying addition to any broth-based soup. For these to stay firm, make sure you lower the heat to the lowest of low—barely a simmer. Then gently drop the tablespoons of batter on top, cover with the lid, and cook undisturbed for 10 minutes. Try not to peek.

1. In a medium bowl, toss together the flour, cornmeal, baking powder, and salt. With your fingertips, work the broth or butter into the flour until the mixture is crumbly. Using a fork, stir in the milk until blended. Stir in the parsley, season with pepper, and set aside.

2. Drop tablespoons of the dumpling batter in 16 clumps over the top of a low-simmering soup. Cover and simmer until the dumplings are cooked through, about 10 minutes.

3. Ladle the soup into bowls and serve with 2 dumplings each.

Per serving: Calories: 155; Fat: 3g; Saturated fat: 0g; Carbohydrate: 27g; Fiber: 4g; Sugar: 3g; Protein: 7g; Iron: 2mg; Sodium: 347mg

Sweet Potato Black Bean Chili

Serves 4 / Prep time: **15 minutes** / Cook time: **25 minutes**

GLUTEN-FREE, NUT-FREE, SOY-FREE

⅓ cup low-sodium vegetable broth or 2 teaspoons extra-virgin olive oil for sautéing

1 cup chopped onion

3 garlic cloves, chopped

2 teaspoons chili powder, or more to taste

¼ teaspoon salt

Freshly ground black pepper

1 (14.5-ounce) can crushed or diced tomatoes

3 to 4 cups low-sodium vegetable broth

1 cup uncooked lentils

1 (15.5-ounce) can black beans, drained and rinsed

1 large sweet potato, peeled and chopped into ½-inch pieces

This thick, rich, slightly sweet chili is about to become your winter favorite. As with most chili, if you don't have an ingredient, you can simply substitute something else or leave it out. And make it as spicy or mild as you like.

1. In large saucepan over medium-high heat, heat the broth or oil for sautéing. Add the onion and sauté until soft and translucent, 3 to 5 minutes. Add the garlic and chili powder, and season with salt and pepper. Cook for another minute.

2. Add the tomatoes and 3 cups vegetable broth. Add the lentils and bring to a boil. Lower the heat to a simmer and cook on low for about 20 minutes, adding more broth if necessary. The lentils should be almost cooked.

3. Add the black beans and sweet potato. Add more broth if needed. Simmer for another 10 minutes or until the sweet potato is soft.

4. Taste and season with salt, pepper, and more chili powder, if needed.

Serving Suggestion: For extra lusciousness, add a dollop of Cashew Sour Cream (see page 151) on top.

Per serving: Calories: 335; Fat: 1g; Saturated fat: 0g; Carbohydrate: 60g; Fiber: 24g; Sugar: 6g; Protein: 22g; Iron: 6mg; Sodium: 258mg

CHAPTER 5

Sandwiches and Burgers

← —— Maple Tofu Bacon and Roasted Tomato Sandwich, p.82

Chipotle Beans and Avocado Toast

Serves 4 / Prep time: 10 minutes

NUT-FREE, OIL-FREE, SOY-FREE

1 (15.5-ounce) can red kidney beans, drained, rinsed, and mashed

1 chipotle in adobo sauce, finely chopped, plus a bit of the sauce

Freshly ground black pepper

Salt

2 avocados, sliced

4 vegan bread slices, toasted

¼ cup thinly sliced radishes

Switch up your avocado toast by adding high-protein chipotles and kidney beans. The chipotles in adobo sauce add a smoky, complex taste to this filling, healthy dish. Beans are one of the healthiest foods you can eat; they are low in calories and high in fiber and protein, helping slow the absorption of carbohydrates from the food and thereby reduce blood sugar levels. Feel free to switch it up with black beans or any beans you prefer.

1. In a medium mixing bowl, add the mashed kidney beans and the chipotle with a bit of adobo sauce. Lightly season with pepper and a tiny bit of salt.

2. Layer the avocado slices on the toasted bread. Top with the chipotle-bean mixture and radish slices.

Serving Suggestion: The radish slices add beautiful color and a crunchy, spicy, peppery texture. The secret is to slice them paper thin.

Per serving: Calories: 333; Fat: 16g; Saturated fat: 2g; Carbohydrate: 39g; Fiber: 14g; Sugar: 2g; Protein: 13g; Iron: 4mg; Sodium: 226mg

Sundried Tomato and Chickpea Sandwich

Serves 4 / Prep time: 10 minutes

GLUTEN-FREE, NUT-FREE, SOY-FREE

1 cup sundried tomatoes, chopped

½ cup vegan mayonnaise or Tofu Mayonnaise (page 150)

½ cup chopped fresh basil

2 (15.5-ounce) cans low-sodium chickpeas, drained and rinsed

Salt

Freshly ground black pepper

8 vegan bread slices or 4 vegan buns, toasted

This is one of my favorite sandwiches. Sundried tomatoes have an intense sweet-tart flavor that is much richer and tangier than fresh tomatoes. Chickpeas make a great base for any sandwich. They're a staple in cuisines around the world, from garbanzos in Spanish-speaking countries to ceci in Italy to chana in India.

1. In a food processor, add the tomatoes, mayonnaise, and basil and process until smooth.

2. Add the chickpeas and process another 10 to 15 seconds. The chickpeas should still be lumpy but somewhat mashed up.

3. Transfer everything to a large bowl and stir to combine. Season with salt and pepper.

4. Spread the mixture on your favorite toasted vegan bread.

Ingredient Tip: The sundried tomatoes need some moisture. You can buy them packed in oil or soak them in boiling water for 15 minutes to soften.

Per serving: Calories: 304; Fat: 10g; Saturated fat: 1g; Carbohydrate: 44g; Fiber: 6g; Sugar: 11g; Protein: 12g; Iron: 6mg; Sodium: 589mg

White Bean, Artichoke Heart, and Spinach Stuffed Pita

Serves 4 / Prep time: **10 minutes**

NUT-FREE, OIL-FREE, SOY-FREE

3 tablespoons fresh lemon juice, divided

2 cups mashed cooked white beans

Salt

Freshly ground black pepper

8 whole-wheat pitas

1½ cups chopped canned artichoke hearts, drained

2 cups baby spinach

White beans mash easily into a creamy texture, making them the perfect base for any sandwich. The tangy artichokes add a delicate sweetness. And there are so many reasons to love artichokes, which are a variety of thistle. The part we eat is actually the immature flower bud. They have an amazing flavor and are loaded with potassium, a mineral that helps maintain normal heart rhythm and controls blood pressure.

1. In a medium bowl, combine 2 tablespoons of lemon juice with the white beans. Season lightly with salt and pepper.

2. Stuff the pitas about a third of the way with the white bean mixture, then add the artichoke hearts and baby spinach. Drizzle the filling with the remaining 1 tablespoon lemon juice.

Substitution Tip: Add ¼ cup hemp seeds to the bean mixture for added protein and omega-3s.

Per serving: Calories: 298; Fat: 2g; Saturated fat: 0g; Carbohydrate: 59g; Fiber: 15g; Sugar: 2g; Protein: 14g; Iron: 4mg; Sodium: 551mg

Savory Tempeh Wraps

Serves 4 / Prep time: **10 minutes, plus time to marinate** / Cook time: **24 minutes**

NUT-FREE, OIL-FREE

1 (8-ounce) package tempeh

3 tablespoons low-sodium soy sauce or tamari

2 tablespoons Dijon mustard

2 tablespoons pure maple syrup

1 tablespoon chopped garlic

2 tablespoons water

4 whole-wheat tortilla wraps

The hot, creamy, and super-sharp taste of the Dijon mustard marinade takes this tempeh wrap to the next level. If you have never used tempeh before, I highly recommend trying it. Tempeh is a traditional Indonesian protein made from fermented soybeans. Following fermentation, the soybeans are pressed into a compact cake. Tempeh has a dry and firm, but chewy, texture and a slightly nutty taste, and is incredibly nutritious. One cup contains 31 grams of protein. Although tempeh isn't as popular as tofu, it is a wonderful substitute for meat.

1. Cut the tempeh into 8 rectangles.

2. In a medium bowl, whisk together the soy sauce, mustard, maple syrup, garlic, and water. Add the tempeh to the marinade and toss to coat. Cover and refrigerate for at least 2 to 3 hours or overnight.

3. Preheat the oven to 375°F. Line a large baking sheet with parchment paper.

4. Add the marinated tempeh slices (reserve the remaining marinade). Bake for 12 minutes, flip over, and bake for another 12 minutes.

5. Coat the tempeh with the remaining marinade and roll up in the tortilla wraps to serve.

continued →

Savory Tempeh Wraps *continued*

Serving Tip: Add any of your favorite ingredients to the wrap, including sliced avocado and crunchy greens. Or make a TLT by adding tomatoes, lettuce, and Tofu Mayonnaise (see page 150).

Per serving: Calories: 318; Fat: 11g; Saturated fat: 2g; Carbohydrate: 41g; Fiber: 4g; Sugar: 9g; Protein: 18g; Iron: 966mg; Sodium: 2mg

Cauliflower Egg Salad Sandwich

Serves 4 / Prep time: 15 minutes, plus 30 minutes to chill

GLUTEN-FREE, NUT-FREE, OIL-FREE, SOY-FREE

1 small to medium
  cauliflower head

¼ cup nutritional yeast

½ cup plus
  2 tablespoons
  vegan mayonnaise
  or Tofu Mayonnaise
  (page 150)

¼ cup fresh lemon juice

1 tablespoon plus
  1 teaspoon
  yellow mustard

¼ **teaspoon salt**

**Freshly ground
  black pepper**

½ **cup chopped
  red onion**

Cauliflower stands in for hardboiled eggs in this creamy cauliflower sandwich. It has a rich flavor and all the taste and mouthfeel of traditional egg salad, without all the cholesterol. This is the basic recipe, but don't hesitate to add your favorite traditional egg salad components. Try adding ½ cup chopped celery or some deviled egg standards like a handful of chopped dill and a sprinkling of paprika. Serve on whole-wheat vegan bread with lettuce, tomato, and bean sprouts.

1. Grate the cauliflower on a box grater with the large holes or chop into small pieces. You should end up with about 4 cups.

2. In a large bowl, whisk together the nutritional yeast, mayonnaise, lemon juice, mustard, salt, and a little pepper.

3. Add the cauliflower and onion. Stir to combine. Taste and add more salt and pepper, if needed.

4. Refrigerate, covered, for 30 minutes to 1 hour, so the flavors can meld.

continued →

Cauliflower Egg Salad Sandwich *continued*

Preparation Tip: To prepare the cauliflower, rinse and remove the slight discolorations with a vegetable peeler. Pat the cauliflower dry. Trim the stalk, removing the core and outer leaves. Break into flowerets, discard the inner core, and chop or grate.

Per serving: Calories: 179; Fat: 9g; Saturated fat: 0g; Carbohydrate: 19g; Fiber: 8g; Sugar: 4g; Protein: 11g; Iron: 1mg; Sodium: 476mg

Jackfruit Barbecue Sandwich

Serves 4 / **Prep time: 10 minutes** / **Cook time: 35 minutes**

SOY-FREE, GLUTEN-FREE, NUT-FREE

- 2 (14-ounce) cans green jackfruit packed in brine or water
- **⅓ cup low-sodium vegetable broth or 2 teaspoons extra-virgin olive oil for sautéing**
- **4 garlic cloves, minced**
- 1 tablespoon grated fresh ginger
- 1 teaspoon ground chipotle or chili powder
- **Freshly ground black pepper**
- 1 cup barbecue sauce, or more to taste
- **¼ to ½ cup water**
- 4 vegan buns, toasted

Jackfruit is increasingly being used as a plant-based meat alternative because it soaks up flavor and has a stringy, meat-like texture. Before it fully ripens, it has a neutral flavor and works well in savory dishes like barbecue. Jackfruit is packed with nutrients, including fiber, vitamin C, phytonutrients, and antioxidants. It's particularly high in vitamin B6, which is important for heart health, brain development, and energy.

1. Drain and rinse the jackfruit. Then squeeze out the extra water and shred the jackfruit with your hands.

2. In a nonstick pan over medium heat, heat the broth or oil for sautéing. Add the jackfruit, garlic, ginger, chipotle, and pepper. Cook, stirring, for 4 to 5 minutes.

3. Add the barbecue sauce and ¼ cup water and mix well. Bring to a simmer.

4. Simmer for 30 minutes, stirring every 10 minutes and adding more water if needed. The jackfruit should be fork-tender.

5. Spoon onto toasted buns to serve.

Per serving: Calories: 285; Fat: 2g; Saturated fat: 0g; Carbohydrate: 58g; Fiber: 11g; Sugar: 16g; Protein: 6g; Iron: 7mg; Sodium: 840mg

Maple Tofu Bacon and Roasted Tomato Sandwich

Serves 4 / Prep time: **10 minutes, plus 1 hour to marinate** / Cook time: **30 minutes**

NUT-FREE, OIL-FREE

¼ cup pure maple syrup

2 tablespoons soy sauce or tamari

1 (16-ounce) package extra-firm tofu or tempeh, thinly sliced

4 cups cherry tomatoes, halved

8 vegan whole-wheat or sourdough bread slices, toasted

Freshly ground black pepper

The roasted tomatoes are the star of this show, and the maple tofu bacon adds a smoky depth. You can substitute thinly sliced eggplant or mushrooms, prepared the same way. Just make sure the slices are thin enough to get a little crisp. Try this with some vegan mayonnaise or Tofu Mayonnaise (see page 150).

1. In a small bowl, prepare the marinade by combining the maple syrup and soy sauce. If you're using tofu, drain and squeeze it to remove as much moisture as possible.

2. Add the tofu or tempeh slices to a rectangular dish and pour the marinade over it, making sure all the slices are covered. Cover and marinate in the refrigerator for at least 1 hour or overnight.

3. Preheat the oven to 400°F. Line a rimmed baking sheet with parchment paper.

4. Remove the tempeh or tofu from the marinade and arrange on half the sheet. Spread out the tomatoes on the other half in a single layer.

5. Roast for about 30 minutes, until the tempeh or tofu is crispy and the tomatoes are shrunken.

6. Divide the tofu or tempeh and roasted tomatoes on 4 bread slices. Season with pepper and top with the other slice of bread.

Preparation Tip: Whenever you're cooking tofu, drain the tofu, then wrap the block in paper towels and press under something heavy (such as a cast iron frying pan) to squeeze out as much water as possible without mashing it. This makes the crispiest slices.

Per serving: Calories: 351; Fat: 9g; Saturated fat: 1g; Carbohydrate: 55g; Fiber: 3g; Sugar: 17g; Protein: 19g; Iron: 4mg; Sodium: 691mg

Chickpea and Sweet Potato Burgers

Serves 4 / Prep time: **10 minutes** / Cook time: **25 minutes**

NUT-FREE, OIL-FREE, SOY-FREE

1 large baked
 sweet potato

½ cup cooked mashed
 chickpeas

¼ cup roasted red bell
 peppers, diced

2 garlic cloves, minced

**3 tablespoons
 minced onion**

½ teaspoon
 ground cumin

½ teaspoon salt

**Freshly ground
 black pepper**

¼ cup old-fashioned
 rolled oats

Here is a hearty, healthy, and delicious take on a veggie burger. Sweet potatoes and chickpeas are a powerful duo of flavor and nutrients. Chickpeas provide a variety of health benefits, including fiber and protein, which work together to slow digestion and help promote fullness. Do not steam or boil the sweet potato for this recipe, because it will retain too much water.

1. Preheat the oven to 375°F. Line a large baking sheet with parchment paper.

2. Remove the skin from the baked sweet potato and dice the flesh. You should have about 1 cup.

3. In a large mixing bowl, combine the sweet potato, chickpeas, bell peppers, garlic, onion, cumin, salt, and pepper. Mix with your hands to bind.

4. Begin adding the rolled oats a little at a time and mixing well until the burger holds together. Add some extra oats if necessary.

5. Form the mixture into four burger patties and place on baking sheet. Bake 20 minutes, flip, and continue baking for an additional 5 minutes, or until both sides are golden.

Ingredient Tip: Never put sweet potatoes in the refrigerator. Refrigeration changes the structure of the cell walls, making them harder to break down and requiring more time to cook. Instead, store your sweet potatoes in a cool, dark place.

Per serving: Calories: 97; Fat: 1g; Saturated fat: 0g; Carbohydrate: 18g; Fiber: 3g; Sugar: 4g; Protein: 3g; Iron: 1mg; Sodium: 321mg

Black Bean Burgers with Quinoa Breadcrumbs

Serves 4 / Prep time: **10 minutes, plus time to thicken** / Cook time: **30 minutes**

GLUTEN-FREE, NUT-FREE, SOY-FREE

2 tablespoons ground flaxseed

6 tablespoons water

2 (15.5-ounce) cans black beans, drained, rinsed, and patted dry

3 garlic cloves, chopped

¾ cup seeded and chopped red bell pepper

½ to ¾ cup chopped onion

1 teaspoon ground cumin

¾ cup cooked quinoa breadcrumbs or regular breadcrumbs

Salt

Freshly ground black pepper

Extra-virgin olive oil

Creating your own unique version of a plant-based burger is pretty simple. Begin with the essential ingredients: onions, garlic, and flax eggs (see step 1). Then add 2 cups of your favorite vegetables, such as mushrooms or sweet potatoes. Next, add 1 cup of cooked grains and 1½ cups of cooked legumes. Stir in your favorite texture builders and flavors, like nuts and spices. Finally, pick something dry like breadcrumbs or oats to help bind it together. Or try this quinoa version.

1. In a small bowl, combine the ground flaxseed and water to make flax eggs. Put in the refrigerator for 10 minutes to thicken. (The basic ratio for 1 flax egg is 1 tablespoon of ground flaxseed whisked with 3 tablespoons of water.)

2. Add the beans, garlic, bell pepper, onion, cumin, flax eggs, and breadcrumbs to a food processor and process until they're combined but not mushy, about 10 seconds. Season with salt and pepper. Divide the mixture into 4 patties.

3. Heat a large skillet over medium heat and add just enough oil to lightly coat the bottom. Add your burgers. Cook for 4 to 5 minutes, or until they are browned on the bottom, then flip gently. Cook for another 4 or 5 minutes on the other side.

Ingredient Tip: Quinoa breadcrumbs amp up the protein and gives this burger a nuttier flavor, plus they make this recipe gluten-free. To make them, preheat the oven to 375°F. Spread the cooked quinoa on a large rimmed baking sheet, using your hands to break up any clumps. Sprinkle with salt. Bake, tossing a few times, until the grains dry out and become crisp, 20 to 30 minutes. Store extra quinoa breadcrumbs in the refrigerator in an airtight container for 2 to 3 days.

Per serving: Calories: 290; Fat: 7g; Saturated fat: 1g; Carbohydrate: 44g; Fiber: 15g; Sugar: 2g; Protein: 15g; Iron: 4mg; Sodium: 45mg

Roasted Portobello Mushroom Burgers with Sundried Tomato Relish

Serves 4 / Prep time: **20 minutes, plus 15 minutes to marinate** / Cook time: **25 minutes**

NUT-FREE, OIL-FREE, SOY-FREE

½ cup dry packed sundried tomatoes

3 tablespoons fresh lemon juice, divided

¼ cup balsamic vinegar

4 large portobello mushrooms, stemmed and gills removed

Salt

Freshly ground black pepper

4 vegan buns, toasted

Sundried tomatoes add a tangy bite to these earthy mushrooms. The portobello mushrooms are marinated in fruity, tart balsamic vinegar before being roasted to perfection. You can also grill them 3 to 4 minutes on each side. These mushrooms are also a rich source of niacin, which helps metabolize food into energy. Roast some extra sliced vegetables, like red pepper and eggplant, for an even heartier burger.

1. Place the sundried tomatoes in a bowl and cover with boiling water. Let soak for 15 minutes or until softened. Drain and save the water.

2. In a food processor, combine the sundried tomatoes and 1 tablespoon lemon juice. Process until smooth, adding some of the sundried tomato water until you have a smooth consistency. Set aside.

3. In a small glass bowl, combine the remaining 2 tablespoons of lemon juice and the vinegar. Place the mushrooms in a single layer in a large glass dish and pour the marinade over them. Let sit for at least 15 minutes.

4. Meanwhile, preheat the oven to 400°F and line a large baking sheet with parchment paper.

5. Place the mushrooms cap-side up on the baking sheet. Using a pastry brush, brush the remaining marinade in the dish over the mushrooms. Sprinkle with a little salt and pepper. Bake for 15 to 25 minutes or until the mushrooms are soft and sizzling, turning over once about halfway through.

6. Serve on vegan buns topped with the sundried tomato relish.

Preparation Tip: To remove the gills from a portobello mushroom, flip it cap-side down and remove the stem. Then take a spoon and gently scoop out the gills.

Per serving: Calories: 166; Fat: 2g; Saturated fat: 0g; Carbohydrate: 29g; Fiber: 2g; Sugar: 3g; Protein: 8g; Iron: 1mg; Sodium: 424mg

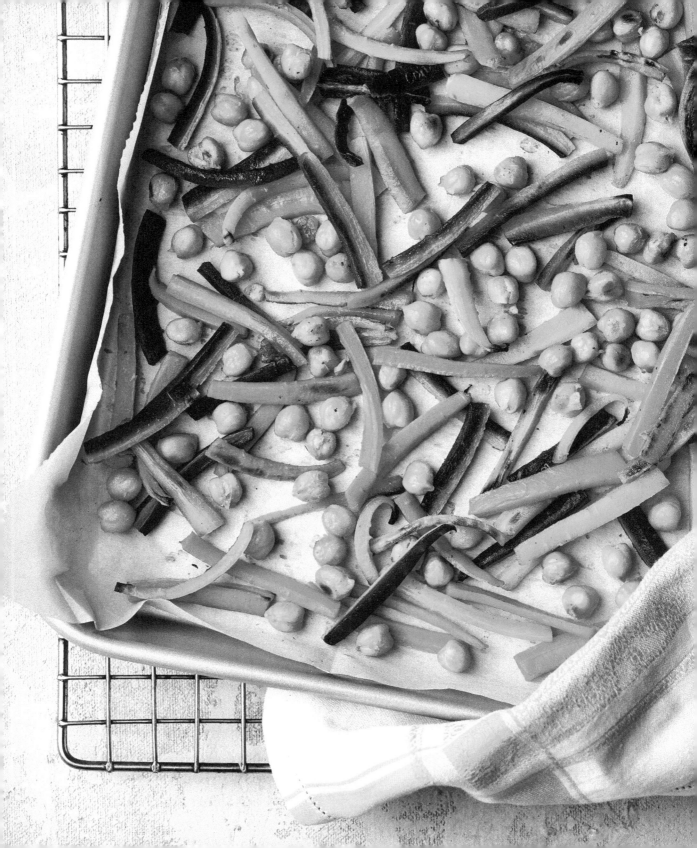

CHAPTER 6

Snacks and Sides

← Roasted Carrots and Chickpeas, p.102

Baked Kale Chips

Serves 2 to 4 / Prep time: 5 minutes / Cook time: 30 minutes

GLUTEN-FREE, NUT-FREE, SOY-FREE

1 bunch large curly or dinosaur (Tuscan) kale

1 tablespoon extra-virgin olive oil

1 teaspoon paprika (optional)

½ teaspoon chili powder (optional)

⅛ teaspoon cayenne pepper (optional)

¼ teaspoon salt

Turn kale leaves into a delicious, healthy snack. These oven-baked treats are easy to prepare, and once you start munching on them, you won't want to stop.

1. Preheat the oven to 300°F. Line two large baking sheets with parchment paper.

2. Rinse and dry the kale, making sure there is no moisture left. Cut away the center spine from each kale leaf and discard. This will leave you with 2 pieces. Cut both pieces in half, so each leaf has been cut into quarters.

3. In a large bowl, combine the salt, oil, and all the spices you are using. Add the kale and massage the oil mixture into the kale with your hands to coat evenly.

4. Arrange the kale pieces in a single layer on the baking sheets and bake until they are crisp, 25 to 30 minutes.

Ingredient Tip: Kale is a bitter green and it needs something to help soften it a bit. An oil or acidic dressing massaged into the kale will help break down the fibers, which will make it easier to chew.

Per serving: Calories: 159; Fat: 7g; Saturated fat: 1g; Carbohydrate: 21g; Fiber: 3g; Sugar: 0g; Protein: 6g; Iron: 3mg; Sodium: 234mg

Avocado Hummus

Serves 4 / Prep time: 10 minutes

GLUTEN-FREE, NUT-FREE, OIL-FREE, SOY-FREE

2 cups cooked chickpeas, drained and rinsed

2 tablespoons Dijon mustard

6 tablespoons tahini

¼ cup water, or more if needed

¼ teaspoon salt

¼ teaspoon freshly ground black pepper

3 ripe avocados, cut into chunks

3 tablespoons fresh lemon juice

This zesty, creamy, vibrant green recipe couldn't be easier or more nutritious. Just place the ingredients in a food processor and whirl away. Avocados are incredibly nutritious and contain more potassium than bananas. They are also loaded with heart-healthy monounsaturated fatty acids and fiber. For a different flavor, skip the avocado and substitute 2 cups of thawed frozen sweet green peas.

1. In a food processor, add the chickpeas, mustard, tahini, water, salt, and pepper and process until smooth. If it's too thick, add a little more water. Scrape into a medium bowl.

2. Without cleaning the processor, add the avocado and lemon juice. Process until smooth.

3. Fold the avocado purée into the chickpea purée and stir. Taste, and season with salt, pepper, and more lemon juice if needed.

Serving Suggestion: Garnish with ¼ cup mixed pomegranate seeds and black poppy seeds and serve with baked pita squares, raw vegetables, or rice cakes.

Per serving: Calories: 493; Fat: 35g; Saturated fat: 5g; Carbohydrate: 39g; Fiber: 18g; Sugar: 5g; Protein: 14g; Iron: 5mg; Sodium: 280mg

White Bean Dip with Olives

Serves 4 / Prep time: 10 minutes

GLUTEN-FREE, NUT-FREE, SOY-FREE

2 (15.5-ounce) cans white beans, drained, rinsed, and coarsely chopped

1 cup pitted mixed olives, coarsely chopped

¼ cup coarsely chopped fresh parsley

1 tablespoon extra-virgin olive oil

3 to 4 tablespoons fresh lemon juice

Zest of 1 lemon, divided

Salt

Freshly ground black pepper

This sophisticated twist on bean dip combines earthy white beans and salty olives and couldn't be healthier or easier to prepare. I like cannellini beans here, but any white beans will do. Substitute navy beans, great northern, or baby lima beans (also known as butter beans). All have similar but distinctive flavors.

1. In a medium bowl, toss the beans, olives, parsley, oil, lemon juice, and most of the lemon zest. Reserve 1 teaspoon of zest for a garnish.

2. Season with salt, pepper, and more lemon juice if desired.

3. Top with the remaining teaspoon of lemon zest to serve.

Serving Suggestion: Sprinkle with red pepper flakes for a little heat. Serve with toasted pita, crackers, vegan baguette slices, or as a dip for vegetables.

Per serving: Calories: 264; Fat: 8g; Saturated fat: 1g; Carbohydrate: 38g; Fiber: 16g; Sugar: 1g; Protein: 12g; Iron: 5mg; Sodium: 336mg

Roasted Eggplant Dip

Serves 4 / Prep time: 10 minutes, plus time to cool and drain / Cook time: 1 hour

GLUTEN-FREE, NUT-FREE, OIL-FREE, SOY-FREE

2 medium eggplants

½ cup tahini

2 tablespoons water

4 teaspoons
    pomegranate
    molasses

3 tablespoons fresh
    lemon juice

6 tablespoons chopped
    fresh parsley

2 garlic cloves, minced

1 teaspoon salt

**Freshly ground
    black pepper**

The secret to this incredible recipe is to cook the eggplant whole, until the skin blisters and blackens. This charring method brings out bold flavors. The pomegranate molasses is tangy and bright in flavor—perhaps unexpectedly sour—and you can use it in dressings and sauces. It's available in most grocery stores or markets that sell Middle Eastern foods. If you don't want to invest in pomegranate molasses, dark molasses is a good substitute, although the flavor is sweeter.

1. Place a rack in the middle of the oven and turn the oven on broil. Line a baking sheet with foil.

2. Pierce the eggplants with a sharp knife in a few places. Put them on the parchment paper-lined baking sheet and place on the middle rack under the broiler. Broil for 45 minutes to 1 hour, turning them every 10 minutes. The eggplants need to deflate completely and the skin should burn and break. Remove the eggplants from the oven and set aside to cool.

continued →

3. When cool enough to handle, cut a slit lengthwise down the center of each eggplant and scoop out the flesh, avoiding the blackened skin, and place in a fine-mesh colander. Leave over a bowl to drain and cool for 40 minutes.

4. Chop the eggplant roughly and transfer to a medium mixing bowl. Add the tahini, water, pomegranate molasses, lemon juice, parsley, garlic, salt, and pepper. Mix well.

5. Taste and season with more salt, pepper, garlic, or lemon juice.

Serving Suggestion: Scatter pomegranate seeds on top and drizzle with a little olive oil, if you're using oil. Serve with toasted pita bread.

Per serving: Calories: 273; Fat: 17g; Saturated fat: 2g; Carbohydrate: 29g; Fiber: 13g; Sugar: 12g; Protein: 8g; Iron: 4mg; Sodium: 630mg

Stuffed Dates with Cashew Cream and Roasted Almonds

Serves 4 / Prep time: **10 minutes, plus 2 hours to soak** / Cook time: **12 minutes**

GLUTEN-FREE, OIL-FREE, SOY-FREE

1 cup shelled, raw, unsalted almonds

2 cups raw unsalted cashews, soaked for 2 hours or overnight, drained and rinsed

1½ tablespoons pure maple syrup

½ teaspoon vanilla extract, or more to taste

¼ cup water, or more as needed

12 fresh dates

This snack is a sweet and savory sensation. The dates contain a fair amount of natural sugar, but they have a low to medium glycemic score, which means they are more slowly absorbed for a slower rise in blood sugar. They are also low in fat and packed with nutrients. Medjool dates are among the most popular varieties, known for their large size and soft skin.

1. Preheat the oven to 350°F. Line a rimmed baking sheet with parchment paper.

2. Spread out the almonds in a single layer and roast for 10 to 12 minutes. Keep a close eye so you don't burn them.

3. In a food processor, add the drained cashews, maple syrup, vanilla, and half of the water. Process until smooth, adding more water if needed.

4. Slice open one side of each date and remove pit with your fingers. Stuff each date with some cashew cream.

5. Serve with roasted almonds.

Per serving: Calories: 646; Fat: 44g; Saturated fat: 6g; Carbohydrate: 49g; Fiber: 9g; Sugar: 22g; Protein: 19g; Iron: 2mg; Sodium: 8mg

Crunchy Vegetable Spring Rolls

Serves 4 / Prep time: 15 minutes

GLUTEN-FREE, NUT-FREE, SOY-FREE

8 (8-inch) dried rice
   paper wrappers

4 cups julienned thin
   crunchy vegetables of
   your choice, like red
   bell pepper, carrots,
   or cucumbers

2 small avocados, sliced

1 small bunch fresh
   mint, stemmed

These flavorful and crunchy spring rolls are as much fun to make as to eat. Ingredients can include cabbage, rice noodles, tofu, and scallions. Basically, you can add whatever you want. Spring rolls have become so popular that you can now find rice paper wrappers in most grocery stores. They are thin, require no cooking, and are made from rice, water, and salt. They also have a nice chewiness.

1. Work with the rice paper 1 wrapper at a time. Pour hot water into a shallow dish and immerse the rice paper sheet to soften, about 15 seconds. Remove from the water and pat both sides dry with a paper towel or clean kitchen towel. Lay on a cutting board.

2. To the bottom third of the wrapper add a small handful of the julienned vegetables, a slice of avocado, and 4 or 5 mint leaves. Gently fold up and over once, then tuck in the edges and continue rolling tightly until the seam is sealed. Set the roll on a platter, seam side down, and cover with a damp kitchen towel.

3. Repeat with the remaining wrappers and ingredients. Serve immediately.

Serving Suggestion: Serve with Sweet and Spicy Peanut Sauce (see page 156) on the side. Or add some thinly sliced tempeh from my Savory Tempeh Wraps recipe (see page 77).

Per serving: Calories: 294; Fat: 14g; Saturated fat: 2g; Carbohydrate: 41g; Fiber: 11g; Sugar: 7g; Protein: 5g; Iron: 4mg; Sodium: 178mg

Coconut Bacon

Serves 4 / Prep time: **5 minutes** / Cook time: **25 minutes**

GLUTEN-FREE, NUT-FREE, OIL-FREE

1½ teaspoons smoked paprika

1½ tablespoons low-sodium, gluten-free soy sauce or tamari

1 tablespoon pure maple syrup

½ teaspoon freshly ground black pepper

½ tablespoon water

3½ cups unsweetened flaked coconut

This coconut bacon is a smoky, crunchy, delicious vegan alternative to traditional bacon, and is wonderful for snacking or topping salads or soups. Coconut is rich in medium-chain triglycerides, which have been dubbed a super fuel because your body absorbs them rapidly and turns them into energy.

1. Preheat the oven to 325°F. Line a large baking sheet with parchment paper.

2. Combine the paprika, soy sauce, maple syrup, pepper, and water in a large bowl.

3. Pour in the flaked coconut and use a wooden spoon to gently toss the coconut in the liquid. When the coconut is evenly coated, pour it onto the baking sheet.

4. Bake for 20 to 25 minutes, using a spatula to flip the bacon about every 5 minutes so it cooks evenly. Keep an eye on it so it doesn't turn too dark and burn. Remove when everything is crispy and golden brown.

Substitution Tip: If you are not a fan of coconut, substitute thin slices of tempeh or tofu.

Per serving: Calories: 204; Fat: 18g; Saturated fat: 16g; Carbohydrate: 12g; Fiber: 5g; Sugar: 7g; Protein: 2g; Iron: 8mg; Sodium: 342mg

Portobello Bacon

Serves 4 / Prep time: 15 minutes, plus overnight to marinate / Cook time: 1 hour

GLUTEN-FREE, OIL-FREE, NUT-FREE

5 large portobello
mushrooms, stemmed
and gills removed

¼ cup gluten-free low-
sodium soy sauce
or tamari

2 teaspoons smoked
paprika

3 tablespoons pure
maple syrup

**Freshly ground
black pepper**

Smoky, savory portobello bacon can make a wonderful replacement for any dish in which you use
traditional bacon. It has the perfect crisp yet
pliant texture and tastes delicious on sandwiches.

1. Cut the mushrooms into ¼-inch slices.

2. In a small bowl, whisk together the soy sauce,
   paprika, and maple syrup. Season with pepper.

3. Place the mushrooms into a shallow glass
   dish and pour the marinade over them. Toss
   to make sure that all the mushroom slices are
   fully covered. Let the mushrooms marinate
   overnight covered in the refrigerator.

4. Preheat the oven to 275°F. Line a baking sheet
   with parchment paper.

5. Lay each mushroom slice on the baking sheet,
   avoiding overlapping. You may need 2 baking
   sheets. Bake for 50 minutes to 1 hour, or
   until crisp.

Tool Tip: Nothing streamlines daily cooking prep like
an inexpensive mandoline slicer, especially when you need
perfectly even, thin slices, as with these mushrooms. Be sure
to buy one with a safety hand guard, and always use it.

Per serving: Calories: 76; Fat: 0g; Saturated fat: 0g;
Carbohydrate: 16g; Fiber: 2g; Sugar: 9g; Protein: 5g; Iron: 1mg;
Sodium: 555mg

Roasted Carrots and Chickpeas

Serves 4 / Prep time: **10 minutes** / Cook time: **30 minutes**

GLUTEN-FREE, NUT-FREE, SOY-FREE

10 carrots, peeled and cut into 1½-inch matchsticks

2 tablespoons fresh lemon juice, divided

3 teaspoons extra-virgin olive oil, divided

¼ teaspoon cayenne pepper or paprika

1½ cups cooked chickpeas

2 teaspoons pure maple syrup

The combination of sweet carrots and crunchy chickpeas makes this vegan snack irresistible. The sweet and tart dressing marries all the flavors. Carrots are crunchy, tasty, and highly nutritious. They are a particularly good source of beta carotene, which gives them their red-orange pigment. Beta carotene is a precursor of vitamin A, which we need for healthy skin and for our immune system.

1. Preheat the oven to 400°F. Line a large baking sheet with parchment paper.

2. Spread out the carrot sticks on the baking sheet and roast for 10 minutes.

3. Meanwhile, in a medium bowl, combine 1 tablespoon of lemon juice, 2 teaspoons of oil, and the cayenne pepper. Toss the chickpeas with the lemon juice mixture.

4. Add to the baking sheet with the carrots and roast for 20 to 30 minutes more, or until the carrots are tender crisp and lightly brown and the chickpeas are crunchy.

5. Meanwhile, whisk together the remaining 1 tablespoon lemon juice, maple syrup, and the 1 teaspoon of oil in a small bowl.

6. Put the carrots and chickpeas in a serving bowl while still warm and toss with the dressing.

Serving Suggestion: Add pita strips during the last 10 minutes of baking for more crunch.

Per serving: Calories: 204; Fat: 5g; Saturated fat: 1g; Carbohydrate: 34g; Fiber: 9g; Sugar: 13g; Protein: 7g; Iron: 2mg; Sodium: 111mg

Cauliflower Buffalo Wings

Serves 4 / Prep time: **10 minutes** / Cook time: **30 minutes**

NUT-FREE

2 tablespoons extra-virgin olive oil

2 tablespoons soy sauce

2 tablespoons rice vinegar

1 to 2 tablespoons sriracha sauce

1 cauliflower head, leaves removed, cut into florets

Chopped fresh cilantro

These spicy, tangy buffalo cauliflower bites are the ultimate meatless hot "wing." Cauliflower is a cruciferous vegetable that is naturally high in fiber, vitamin K, and B vitamins. It also contains antioxidants that help prevent cancer cells and reduce oxidative stress. Serve these hot wings with some cooling Cashew Sour Cream (see page 151) on the side.

1. Preheat the oven to 400°F. Line a large baking sheet with parchment paper.

2. In a large bowl, combine the oil, soy sauce, vinegar, and sriracha sauce.

3. Gently add the cauliflower to the bowl and toss to coat with the marinade.

4. Arrange the cauliflower on a baking sheet and roast for 15 minutes. Turn and roast for another 10 to 15 minutes, or until tender.

5. Garnish with fresh cilantro and serve.

Substitution Tip: People who are using blood thinners should not suddenly start eating a lot of cauliflower because the high levels of vitamin K could react adversely with the drugs. You can use chunks of seitan instead of cauliflower and these will still be delicious.

Per serving: Calories: 123; Fat: 7g; Saturated fat: 1g; Carbohydrate: 12g; Fiber: 5g; Sugar: 5g; Protein: 5g; Iron: 1mg; Sodium: 704mg

Crispy Crunchy Coconut Tofu

Serves 4 / Prep time: **10 minutes** / Cook time: **30 minutes**

NUT-FREE, OIL-FREE

1 (14-ounce) package
  extra-firm tofu

4 tablespoons
  cornstarch

¼ teaspoon
  baking powder

½ teaspoon salt

4 tablespoons water

½ cup panko
  breadcrumbs

Freshly ground
  black pepper

¾ cup unsweetened
  shredded coconut

Treat your taste buds to the crispy coconut flavors of this easy baked tofu. This dish can be enjoyed as a snack, on a salad, or as a meal on its own. Panko breadcrumbs are larger, and I use them here because the flakes tend to stay crisper longer than standard breadcrumbs. But you can use either. If you are soy-free, you can substitute cauliflower florets and cook them the same way.

1. Preheat the oven to 400°F. Line a large baking sheet with parchment paper.

2. Press the tofu with a clean kitchen towel to remove the water, then cut it into 2-inch cubes. In a large bowl, prepare the batter by combining the cornstarch, baking powder, salt, and water in a mixing bowl. The texture will be on the thicker side, like a pancake batter. If it's too thick, add more water.

3. Put the breadcrumbs, salt, pepper, and the shredded coconut on a large plate and use your hands to combine them.

4. Coat each piece of tofu in the batter, then lift to let the excess run off. Dip in the coconut panko breadcrumbs and roll to cover completely. Transfer to the baking sheet.

5. Bake 25 to 30 minutes, or until golden brown.

continued →

Crispy Crunchy Coconut Tofu *continued*

Serving Suggestion: Serve with Smoky Rich Cheese Sauce (see page 162) or Sweet and Spicy Peanut Sauce (see page 156).

Per serving: Calories: 223; Fat: 13g; Saturated fat: 7g; Carbohydrate: 16g; Fiber: 3g; Sugar: 2g; Protein: 11g; Iron: 2mg; Sodium: 339mg

Sweet Potato Latkes

Serves 4 / Prep time: **20 minutes** / Cook time: **10 minutes**

GLUTEN-FREE, NUT-FREE, SOY-FREE

2 sweet potatoes (about 1½ pounds total), peeled

2 russet potatoes (about 1½ pounds total), peeled

1 small red or white onion

Salt

Freshly ground black pepper

2 flax eggs (see Ingredient Tip)

3 tablespoons rice flour

2 teaspoons extra-virgin olive oil

Traditional latkes get an upgrade of antioxidants and sweetness with the addition of sweet potatoes. If you have never had latkes, they are fried white potato pancakes, often flavored with onion. These latkes pair deliciously with a side of apple sauce and Cashew Sour Cream (see page 151).

1. Using the large holes on a box grater (or the large shredding blade of a food processor), grate the sweet potatoes, potatoes, and onion into a large bowl.

2. Wrap everything in a clean dish towel and twist tightly over the sink to wring out as much water as possible.

3. Put the potatoes back in the large bowl and season with salt and pepper. Fold in the flax eggs and rice flour. Combine with your hands until the mixture binds together and everything is thoroughly combined.

4. Place a large nonstick skillet over medium heat. Add the oil and heat until hot.

5. Working in batches, spoon about ¼ cup of the potato mixture into the pan, pressing lightly with a spatula to form 5-inch pancakes that are about ¼-inch thick. Cook until crispy and golden, about 8 minutes, turning once about halfway through.

continued →

Sweet Potato Latkes *continued*

6. Transfer the cooked latkes to the oven to keep warm as you cook more.

Ingredient Tip: The basic ratio for one flax egg is 1 tablespoon of ground flaxseed whisked with 3 tablespoons of water. Place in the refrigerator for 10 minutes to thicken.

Per serving: Calories: 318; Fat: 3g; Saturated fat: 0g; Carbohydrate: 69g; Fiber: 10g; Sugar: 10g; Protein: 6g; Iron: 2mg; Sodium: 143mg

Italian-Style Spaghetti Squash

Serves 4 / Prep time: 10 minutes / Cook time: 45 minutes

GLUTEN-FREE, NUT-FREE, SOY-FREE

1 large spaghetti
squash (about
2½ pounds), halved
lengthwise, seeded
and membranes
removed

**2 tablespoons extra-
virgin olive oil**

**Freshly ground
black pepper**

¼ cup pine nuts

2 cups tomato sauce

This simple side dish can be served with just about anything. It's the ultimate healthy alternative to regular pasta. Spaghetti squash is also a nutrient-dense food, meaning it is low in calories but high in vitamins, minerals, and fiber. The cooked strands make a delicious low-carb base for pad Thai or a stir-fry. Or you can serve them with my Sunday Gravy with Tomatoes and Carrots (see page 166).

1. Preheat the oven to 425°F. Line a 9-by-13-inch baking dish with parchment paper.

2. Drizzle the flesh of the squash with oil and season with pepper. If you are oil-free, omit oil. Place the squash in the baking dish cut-side down and roast until golden and tender when pierced with knife, about 45 minutes.

3. Meanwhile, grind the pine nuts in a small food processor or spice grinder.

4. When the squash is cooked and cool enough to handle, use a fork to scrape the flesh toward the center to create long strands. Put the strands into a large bowl.

continued →

5. Warm the tomato sauce in a medium saucepan or the microwave. To serve, pour a ½ cup of tomato sauce in the center of each plate. Using tongs, twirl one-quarter of the spaghetti squash tightly and mound on top of the sauce. Top each serving with 1 tablespoon of ground pine nuts.

Substitution Tip: Replace spaghetti squash with spiraled butternut squash or sweet potato.

Per serving: Calories: 205; Fat: 11g; Saturated fat: 1g; Carbohydrate: 27g; Fiber: 2g; Sugar: 6g; Protein: 5g; Iron: 3mg; Sodium: 693mg

Roasted Brussels Sprouts with Warm Maple Sauce

Serves 4 / Prep time: **15 minutes** / Cook time: **30 minutes**

GLUTEN-FREE, NUT-FREE, SOY-FREE

1 pound (about 30) small Brussels sprouts, trimmed and halved

1 tablespoon extra-virgin olive oil

¼ teaspoon salt, plus a pinch, divided

Freshly ground black pepper

¼ cup pure maple syrup

2½ tablespoons sherry or red wine vinegar

¾ teaspoon crushed red pepper flakes

Roasting gives these Brussels sprouts a caramelized, nutty flavor, and the maple syrup sauce adds a beautiful hint of smoky sweetness. Ultra-flavorful and crispy, they make the perfect side dish for any meal. Brussels sprouts contain glucosinolates, and a number of studies suggest that a diet rich in glucosinolates may lower your risk of certain cancers.

1. Heat the oven to 450°F. Line a rimmed baking sheet with parchment paper.

2. In a large bowl, toss the Brussels sprouts with the oil. If you are oil-free, omit oil. Season with a pinch salt and pepper. Arrange the Brussels sprouts, cut-side down, on the baking sheet. Roast until tender and browned, 20 to 25 minutes.

3. Meanwhile, in a saucepan over medium heat, bring the maple syrup to a simmer. Reduce the heat to low and cook, stirring often, for about 3 minutes. Whisk in the vinegar, the remaining ¼ teaspoon of salt, and the red pepper flakes and cook, whisking constantly, for another 3 minutes.

continued →

4. Transfer the cooked Brussels sprouts to a large bowl. Add the sauce and toss to coat.

Ingredient Tip: Store fresh, unwashed, untrimmed Brussels sprouts in a bag in the crisper drawer of your refrigerator. Remove any yellowed or wilted leaves first.

Per serving: Calories: 132; Fat: 4g; Saturated fat: 1g; Carbohydrate: 24g; Fiber: 4g; Sugar: 14g; Protein: 4g; Iron: 2mg; Sodium: 178mg

CHAPTER 7

Entrées

← *Cauliflower Steaks with Pear Curry Chutney, p.122*

Harvest Moon Stew with Squash, Pinto Beans, and Corn

Serves 4 / Prep time: **15 minutes** / Cook time: **30 minutes**

GLUTEN-FREE, NUT-FREE, SOY-FREE

⅓ cup vegetable broth or 2 teaspoons extra-virgin olive oil for sautéing

1½ cups chopped onion

4 garlic cloves, chopped

1 butternut squash, peeled, halved, seeded, and cut into ½-inch cubes (about 4½ cups)

1 (15.5-ounce) can pinto beans, drained and rinsed

2 cups water or low-sodium vegetable broth

3½ cups fresh or frozen corn kernels

1 teaspoon salt

Freshly ground black pepper

1 cup coarsely chopped fresh basil

This seriously satisfying and hearty stew is filled to the brim with delicious vegetables and buttery beans. Pintos are one of my favorite beans. They are small but flavorful and are a central part of the cuisines of many Latin American countries. Pinto beans also make the best refried beans. Butternut squash adds a nutty, sweet taste and a lovely texture to this autumnal stew.

1. In a medium saucepan over medium heat, heat the oil. Add the onion and cook until soft and translucent, 3 to 4 minutes. Add the garlic and cook for another minute.

2. Add the squash, beans, and water. Bring to a boil, then lower the heat to a simmer and cook for 15 minutes. Add the corn and cook another 10 minutes, or until the squash is tender.

3. Add the salt and season with pepper. Stir in the chopped basil and serve.

Per serving: Calories: 321; Fat: 4g; Saturated fat: 1g; Carbohydrate: 68g; Fiber: 13g; Sugar: 10g; Protein: 12g; Iron: 3mg; Sodium: 592mg

Cabbage Roll Stew

Serves 4 to 6 / Prep time: **10 minutes** / Cook time: **30 minutes**

NUT-FREE, SOY-FREE

2 (8-ounce) packages seitan, cubed

¼ cup all-purpose flour

¼ **teaspoon salt, plus a pinch, divided**

Freshly ground black pepper

⅓ **cup low-sodium vegetable broth or 2 teaspoons extra-virgin olive oil for sautéing**

1 cup chopped onion

3 garlic cloves, chopped

1 small green cabbage, cored and coarsely chopped (about 8 cups)

2 cups low-sodium vegetable broth

2 (14.5-ounce) cans low-sodium diced tomatoes

1 cup raisins

I've put all the delicious ingredients of a stuffed cabbage roll in a rich and hearty stew. Cabbage can keep inflammation in check and is an excellent source of vitamin K, which aids bone health and wound healing. Seitan is a protein made from wheat gluten, popular in the vegan world for its chewy, meat-like texture and protein.

1. In a large bowl, toss the seitan with the flour. Season with a pinch salt and pepper.

2. In a large saucepan over medium-high heat, heat the broth or oil for sautéing. Add the seitan and brown for 5 minutes. Remove from the pan and set aside.

3. Add the onion and cook until soft and translucent, 3 to 5 minutes. Add the garlic and cook for another minute. Add the chopped cabbage, 2 cups vegetable broth, the remaining 1 teaspoon salt, pepper, and tomatoes. Bring to a boil, then simmer for 15 minutes.

4. Add the raisins and cooked seitan. Add more vegetable broth if needed. Cook for another 5 minutes, then adjust the seasonings.

Per serving: Calories: 369; Fat: 2g; Saturated fat: 1g; Carbohydrate: 57g; Fiber: 11g; Sugar: 34g; Protein: 32g; Iron: 3mg; Sodium: 637mg

One-Pot Chickpea, Sweet Potato, and Cauliflower Stew

Serves 4 / Prep time: **10 minutes** / Cook time: **30 minutes**

GLUTEN-FREE, NUT-FREE, SOY-FREE

⅓ cup low-sodium vegetable broth or 2 teaspoons extra-virgin olive oil for sautéing

¾ cup chopped onion

½ tablespoon chili powder

1 sweet potato, peeled and cut into bite-size pieces (about 2 cups)

4 cups chopped cauliflower

1 (15.5-ounce) can chickpeas, drained and rinsed

1 (14.5-ounce) can diced tomatoes

2½ to 3 cups low-sodium vegetable broth

½ teaspoon salt

Freshly ground black pepper

This enticingly delicious stew is made with simple, nutrient-dense, low-fat ingredients. Everything cooks in one pot for maximum flavor and minimum cleanup. One-pot meals nearly always contain a starch, a protein, and a vegetable all rolled into one happy pot of food. Don't be afraid to be creative and switch up the ingredients.

1. In a large saucepan over medium heat, heat the broth or oil for sautéing. Add the onion and cook until soft and translucent, 3 to 5 minutes, adding more vegetable broth if needed.

2. Add the chili powder, sweet potato, cauliflower, chickpeas, tomatoes, and 2½ cups vegetable broth. Bring to a boil and lower the heat to a simmer. Partially cover and cook until the sweet potato is tender, about 25 minutes, adding more vegetable broth if needed.

3. Taste and season with salt and pepper.

Serving Suggestion: Add a light sprinkling of cayenne pepper for some heat. Serve over brown rice with a side of leafy greens.

Per serving: Calories: 195; Fat: 2g; Saturated fat: 0g; Carbohydrate: 37g; Fiber: 10g; Sugar: 11g; Protein: 9g; Iron: 3mg; Sodium: 463mg

Cauliflower Fried Rice

Serves 4 / Prep time: 10 minutes / Cook time: 30 minutes

NUT-FREE

½ cup uncooked
  brown rice

1 cup water

½ cauliflower head

⅓ **cup low-sodium
  vegetable broth
  or 2 teaspoons
  extra-virgin olive oil
  for sautéing**

1 cup chopped onion

2 garlic cloves, chopped

½ **cup frozen peas**

½ **cup frozen corn**

**2 tablespoons soy sauce
  or tamari**

Cauliflower fried rice is an easy and fast Chinese-inspired dish. Not only is it delicious, but it's also protein-packed. Did you know one medium cauliflower head has 11 grams of protein? I recommend adding peas and corn, but this rice is your canvas and any vegetables will work. Add some cubed tofu or tempeh to amp up the protein.

1. Rinse the brown rice under cool water and add to a medium saucepan with the water. Bring to boil and simmer, covered, until all the water is absorbed and the rice is cooked, 20 to 25 minutes. Keep a careful eye on it. When done, remove the cover and let it sit off the heat.

2. Meanwhile, remove the outer leaves of the cauliflower, rinse well, and drain and dry. Grate the cauliflower on the coarse side of a large box grater. This should yield about 3 cups of riced cauliflower.

3. In a large nonstick sauté pan over medium heat, heat the broth or oil for sautéing. Add the onion and cook until soft and translucent, 3 to 5 minutes. Add the garlic and cook for another minute, adding more vegetable broth if the food is sticking.

continued →

Cauliflower Fried Rice *continued*

4. Add the riced cauliflower and cook for 3 minutes. Add the peas and corn and cook for another 3 to 5 minutes. Add the cooked brown rice and soy sauce and cook until heated through.

Preparation Tip: Whatever vegetables you're adding, try to cut them all the same size so they cook in about the same time.

Per serving: Calories: 146; Fat: 1g; Saturated fat: 0g; Carbohydrate: 30g; Fiber: 4g; Sugar: 4g; Protein: 5g; Iron: 2mg; Sodium: 486mg

Glazed Eggplant and Black Sesame Fried Rice

Serves 4 / Prep time: **10 minutes** / Cook time: **10 minutes**

GLUTEN-FREE, NUT-FREE

⅓ **cup low-sodium vegetable broth or 2 teaspoons extra-virgin olive oil or sesame oil for sautéing**

4 large Japanese eggplants, cut into 1-inch strips

½ cup pure maple syrup

½ cup gluten-free, low sodium soy sauce

3 cups cooked black wild rice

½ cup chopped scallions

This dish is all about the earthy, nutty, toasty flavors of the wild rice and the rich umami taste of the Japanese eggplant. Sesame oil adds a nutty, aromatic boost to any Asian-style dish. There are two main kinds of sesame oil: toasted and white. I prefer toasted. You can also make this with portobello mushrooms in place of, or in addition to, the eggplant.

1. In a large sauté pan over medium heat, heat the sesame oil. When it's hot, add the eggplant strips and cook, stirring constantly, until they're soft and golden, about 5 minutes.

2. In a small bowl, combine the maple syrup and soy sauce. Deglaze the sauté pan with the soy-maple mixture. Stir for 1 minute, then add the black rice and stir for 2 to 3 minutes or until the rice is hot.

3. Add the scallions and cook for another minute.

Serving Suggestion: Top with ¼ cup hemp seeds and serve with a side of leafy greens.

Per serving: Calories: 381; Fat: 5g; Saturated fat: 1g; Carbohydrate: 80g; Fiber: 17g; Sugar: 38g; Protein: 11g; Iron: 3mg; Sodium: 1125mg

Cauliflower Steaks with Pear Curry Chutney

Serves 4 / Prep time: 15 minutes / Cook time: 15 minutes

GLUTEN-FREE, NUT-FREE, SOY-FREE

2 tablespoons curry powder

2 medium pears, cored and chopped

1 tablespoon extra-virgin olive oil, divided

½ cup diced red onion

1 large cauliflower head, cut into four ¾-inch to 1-inch steaks

3 tablespoons sherry vinegar

¼ teaspoon salt

Freshly ground black pepper

This recipe has just a few ingredients but a big payoff. Cauliflower steaks are a quick, healthy dinner that can be served with any traditional sides. I love to serve them over quinoa with a side of leafy greens. The pear chutney is a chunky, sweet, savory condiment with a delicate taste of curry. It pairs perfectly with the cauliflower steaks.

1. In a dry saucepan over medium heat, toast the curry powder for about 30 seconds or until it is fragrant. Add the pears, 1 tablespoon of oil, and the onion. Cook, stirring the mixture occasionally, until tender, about 5 minutes. Stir in the vinegar, salt, and pepper, then remove from the heat and set aside.

2. Bring a large pot of lightly salted water to a boil. Carefully, lower the 4 (or more) cauliflower steaks into the water, one by one, using a pair of tongs. Lower the heat to a simmer and cook until just tender, about 8 minutes, being careful not to overcook. The steaks should still have bite. If a paring knife can pierce through the center fairly easily, the steaks should be done.

3. Carefully remove the steaks with a large slotted spoon or skimmer and transfer to a rack to cool. When the steaks are cool, season each with a pinch salt and pepper.

4. Heat a large nonstick skillet over high heat. Add the remaining ½ tablespoon of oil. Carefully sear each cauliflower steak over high heat until browned evenly, about 2 minutes on each side. Season with a little salt and pepper.

5. Place each cauliflower steak on a plate and spoon the chutney over. Serve immediately.

Preparation Tip: You can also bake the cauliflower steaks by placing them on a baking sheet. Lightly coat them with olive oil, salt, pepper, and a sprinkle of crushed red pepper flakes (or add your favorite seasonings). Roast at 400°F for 30 minutes, turning over halfway through, until tender and golden.

Per serving: Calories: 181; Fat: 8g; Saturated fat: 1g; Carbohydrate: 28g; Fiber: 9g; Sugar: 14g; Protein: 5g; Iron: 2mg; Sodium: 216mg

Grilled Portobello Mushrooms over Cauliflower Mash

Serves 4 / Prep time: **15 minutes** / Cook time: **40 minutes**

GLUTEN-FREE, NUT-FREE, SOY-FREE

1 large cauliflower head, trimmed and cut into florets (about 10 cups)

2 teaspoons extra-virgin olive oil, divided

3½ cup unflavored, unsweetened nondairy milk

¼ teaspoon salt

Pinch ground nutmeg

Freshly ground black pepper

4 large portobello mushrooms, stemmed and gills removed

This dish is inspired by the comfort foods of Sunday suppers I ate growing up—rich, straightforward, and oh-so-satisfying flavors. The juicy and delicious portobello mushrooms take the place of meat, and the cauliflower mash is a fun alternative to mashed potatoes. Serve this dish smothered in my Rich and Savory Mushroom Gravy (see page 164).

1. Preheat the oven to 400°F. Line a large baking sheet with parchment paper.

2. Place the cauliflower florets on the baking sheet and toss with 1 teaspoon of oil. Roast until golden and tender, about 30 minutes.

3. Transfer the roasted cauliflower to a food processor. Add the nondairy milk, salt, and nutmeg, and season with pepper. Purée until smooth, adding more milk if needed.

4. Heat a greased grill pan over medium-high heat.

5. Brush the mushrooms with the remaining 1 teaspoon oil. Season with salt and pepper. Place the portobellos cap-side down on the hottest part of the grill pan. Cook for about 5 minutes or more. Flip to the other side and cook for an additional 3 to 5 minutes or more. They should be soft and juicy, with strong grill marks.

6. Slice the mushrooms and serve immediately over the hot cauliflower mash.

Preparation Tip: You could bake the mushrooms with the cauliflower, but grilling coaxes out the deepest flavors.

Per serving: Calories: 103; Fat: 3g; Saturated fat: 0g; Carbohydrate: 15g; Fiber: 7g; Sugar: 5g; Protein: 8g; Iron: 2mg; Sodium: 255mg

Samosa Patties

Serves 4 / Prep time: **5 minutes** / Cook time: **30 minutes**

GLUTEN-FREE, OIL-FREE, SOY-FREE

1 to 2 cups raw unsalted cashews, ground into course meal

1 cup frozen peas, thawed

1½ cups chopped cauliflower

2 cups peeled and cubed baked russet potato

2 tablespoons curry powder

½ teaspoon salt

Freshly ground black pepper

Traditionally an Indian samosa is a fried or baked pastry filled with a savory filling, such as potatoes and green peas. This is a deeply satisfying healthy baked version. I highly recommend serving these patties with my Pear Curry Chutney (see page 122) and some leafy greens.

1. Preheat the oven to 400°F. Line a large baking sheet with parchment paper.

2. In a large bowl, combine 1 cup of ground cashews, the peas, cauliflower, potato, curry powder, salt, and pepper, pressing the mixture together until it begins to bind. Add more ground cashews as needed until the mixture is well incorporated and bound together.

3. Form into 4 burger-size patties. Place them on the lined baking sheet.

4. Bake for 15 minutes, then flip the patty carefully. Continue baking for another 15 minutes, or until both sides are golden.

Preparation Tip: Steaming or boiling the potato will add too much moisture, so only use baked potato.

Per serving: Calories: 255; Fat: 14g; Saturated fat: 2g; Carbohydrate: 25g; Fiber: 6g; Sugar: 3g; Protein: 9g; Iron: 2mg; Sodium: 337mg

Sesame Peanut Butter Noodles

Serves 4 / Prep time: **5 minutes** / Cook time: **10 minutes**

1 pound spaghetti or
your favorite noodle,
such as soba, rice, or
tofu noodles

2 tablespoons low-
sodium soy sauce
or tamari

½ to 1 tablespoon
sesame oil

¼ cup peanut butter

1 tablespoon sriracha
sauce, or more to taste

These soft and luxurious noodles are bathed in a mixture of sesame oil, peanut butter, and sriracha sauce for heat. Served cold or warm, it's a quick and delicious meal for any time of day. Remember, conventional peanut butter can contain hydrogenated oils, sugar, corn syrup, and salt. Read the label carefully and choose one that has just one or two simple ingredients. You can also substitute any nut butter, or seed butter if you have a nut allergy.

1. Cook the noodles according to the package directions. Drain, but save ½ cup of starch water from the noodles.

2. In a large bowl, whisk together the soy sauce, ½ tablespoon oil, peanut butter, and sriracha. Begin adding a little of the starch water, until the sauce reaches your preferred consistency.

3. Add the noodles to the bowl and toss well to coat. Season with more sesame oil if needed.

Serving Suggestion: Garnish with 3 sliced scallions and 1 teaspoon sesame seeds.

Per serving: Calories: 442; Fat: 3g; Saturated fat: 1g; Carbohydrate: 86g; Fiber: 4g; Sugar: 3g; Protein: 15g; Iron: 2mg; Sodium: 458mg

One-Pot Thai Coconut Curry Rice with Green Beans

Serves 4 / Prep time: **10 minutes** / Cook time: **35 minutes**

GLUTEN-FREE, NUT-FREE, SOY-FREE

⅓ cup low-sodium
vegetable broth
or 1 or 2 teaspoons
extra-virgin olive oil
for sautéing

1 (10-ounce) package
extra-firm tofu or
tempeh, cut into
2-inch cubes

1 teaspoon salt, plus a
pinch, divided

Freshly ground
black pepper

1 (14.5-ounce) can light
coconut milk

1½ cups low-sodium
vegetable broth

½ cup water

1 tablespoon Thai
red curry paste
or 1 tablespoon
curry powder

1 cup uncooked
jasmine rice

2 cups green beans,
stem ends removed,
cut into 1-inch lengths

The combination of Thai red curry and coconut milk creates a creamy, warm, flavorful base for the rice and tofu or tempeh. Both will taste delicious in this recipe, but there are key differences in texture and taste. Tempeh is made from fermented soybeans and is often described as earthy, hearty, or nutty. Tofu, on the other hand, is made from unfermented soy milk that's been processed into solid white blocks. Tofu has a more neutral flavor and absorbs the flavor of all the other ingredients. Either choice has big health benefits, including lots of protein and omega-3 fats.

1. In a 5-quart Dutch oven or heavy pot over medium-high heat, heat the broth or oil for sautéing. Season the tofu or tempeh with a pinch salt and pepper. Working in two batches, cook the tofu or tempeh until it's brown on both sides, 3 to 5 minutes on each side. Transfer to a plate.

2. Add the coconut milk, 1½ cups vegetable broth, water, curry paste, and the remaining 1 teaspoon salt. Bring to a boil and stir in the rice. Cover and reduce the heat to medium-low. Cook without stirring until the rice is almost tender, about 15 minutes.

3. Add the tofu or tempeh chunks on top of the rice. Scatter the green beans on top of the tofu. Cover and cook on low until the vegetables are crisp-tender, about 10 minutes.

Serving Suggestion: You can also make this with brown rice (you will have to extend the cooking time for the rice). Serve with lemon or lime wedges on the side, and garnish with fresh Thai basil.

Per serving: Calories: 316; Fat: 10g; Saturated fat: 4g; Carbohydrate: 48g; Fiber: 5g; Sugar: 4g; Protein: 11g; Iron: 4mg; Sodium: 676mg

Savory Chickpea Pancakes with Arugula Salad

Serves 4 / Prep time: 15 minutes / Cook time: 10 minutes

GLUTEN-FREE, NUT-FREE, SOY-FREE

FOR THE PANCAKES

3 cups chickpea flour

3 cups water

3 tablespoons minced onion

2 tablespoons seeded and chopped jalapeño pepper

2 tablespoons chopped fresh tarragon or cilantro

2 teaspoons extra-virgin olive oil

FOR THE SALAD

2 tablespoons fresh lemon juice

1 tablespoon extra-virgin olive oil

1 (6-ounce) bag arugula

Freshly ground black pepper

These crispy and golden brown chickpea pancakes, known as socca, are a popular street food in the Mediterranean regions of France. You can find these naturally gluten-free flatbreads cooked on outdoor grills, then coarsely chopped and served in a paper cone with a sprinkling of salt and pepper. They are satisfying and a great source of plant-based protein. If you can't find chickpea flour (also known as garbanzo bean flour) at your supermarket, try a health food store or online.

1. In large bowl, whisk together the chickpea flour and water until smooth. Add the onion, jalapeño pepper, and tarragon. Let the batter rest for 10 minutes.

2. While you're waiting, in a large bowl, whisk together the lemon juice and oil for the salad dressing. Add the arugula and toss to coat. Season with pepper.

3. In a large skillet over medium-high heat, heat the oil. When the skillet is hot but not smoking, add ⅓ cup of the batter. Cook the pancake until browned around the edges and set on top, about 3 minutes. Make sure the pancake is completely set before flipping. Turn the pancake over with a spatula and cook for

1 to 3 minutes longer. Transfer to a baking sheet lined with parchment paper. Repeat with remaining pancake batter. Lightly re-oil the skillet if needed.

4. When all the pancakes are cooked, serve the arugula salad over 2 to 3 warm pancakes per person.

Substitution Tip: Replace the white onion in the pancakes with scallions. You can also add chopped black olives and sundried tomatoes to the batter.

Per serving: Calories: 333; Fat: 11g; Saturated fat: 1g; Carbohydrate: 42g; Fiber: 8g; Sugar: 9g; Protein: 17g; Iron: 4mg; Sodium: 639mg

One-Pot Tomato Basil Spinach Pasta

Serves 4 / Prep time: **5 minutes** / Cook time: **10 minutes**

NUT-FREE, OIL-FREE, SOY-FREE

1 (12-ounce) box
   uncooked spaghetti

1 (15.5-ounce) can
   diced tomatoes

1 onion, julienned

**4 garlic cloves,
   thinly sliced**

1 handful fresh basil,
   chopped

**4½ cups low-sodium
   vegetable broth**

2 teaspoons dried
   oregano

½ teaspoon salt

**Freshly ground
   black pepper**

1 handful fresh spinach

When you are craving comfort food but don't want to spend a ton of time in the kitchen, this one-pot dish is the easiest pasta you will ever make. Add ½ cup chopped sundried tomatoes along with everything else for an even deeper flavor.

1. Place the pasta, tomatoes, onion, garlic, and basil in a large soup pot. Pour in the vegetable broth. Sprinkle the dried oregano on top. Add the salt and some pepper.

2. Cover the pot and bring to a boil over medium-high heat. Reduce to a low simmer and cook for 7 or 8 minutes, stirring every 2 minutes.

3. Add the spinach and continue cooking another 2 or 3 minutes, or until there is only about 1 inch of liquid left in the bottom of the pot.

Serving Suggestion: Grind ¼ cup pine nuts for a Parmesan-type topping, and sprinkle each serving with some extra chopped fresh basil.

Per serving: Calories: 376; Fat: 2g; Saturated fat: 0g; Carbohydrate: 74g; Fiber: 6g; Sugar: 7g; Protein: 16g; Iron: 5mg; Sodium: 394mg

Orecchiette with Smoky Pinto Beans

Serves 3 to 4 / Prep time: 15 minutes / Cook time: 15 minutes

NUT-FREE, SOY-FREE

1 cup uncooked orecchiette pasta

½ cup low-sodium vegetable broth or 2 teaspoons extra-virgin olive oil for sautéing

1 cup chopped onion

3 garlic cloves, chopped

1 (15.5-ounce) can pinto beans, drained and rinsed

1 (15.5-ounce) can fire-roasted crushed tomatoes

2 teaspoons ground cumin

½ teaspoon salt

Freshly ground black pepper

1 teaspoon chopped chipotles in adobo sauce

This smoky, flavorful dish is a perfect example of calorie density. It has lots of vegetables and beans to keep you full, and you still get your pasta fix. The fire-roasted tomatoes have a sweet, smoky depth, and the tangy chipotle adds another layer of fiery, smoky flavor. If you like bold flavors, you will enjoy this dish.

1. Cook the orecchiette according to the package directions. Drain and set aside.

2. Meanwhile, in a large sauté pan over medium heat, heat the broth or oil for sautéing. Add the onion and cook until soft and translucent, 3 to 4 minutes. Add the garlic and cook for 1 minute more.

3. Add the pinto beans, tomatoes, cumin, salt, pepper, and chopped chipotles. Bring to a boil and reduce to a simmer. Cook for 15 minutes. Taste and decide if you would like a little more heat; if so, add more chipotles.

4. Add the cooked pasta, combine, and heat through.

Per serving: Calories: 272; Fat: 1g; Saturated fat: 0g; Carbohydrate: 53g; Fiber: 12g; Sugar: 9g; Protein: 11g; Iron: 4mg; Sodium: 647mg

Barley and Squash Pistachio Bowl

Serves 4 / Prep time: 15 minutes / Cook time: 1 hour

SOY-FREE

4 cups (about 2 pounds) butternut squash, peeled, seeded, and cut into 1-inch chunks

⅓ cup low-sodium vegetable broth or 2 teaspoons extra-virgin olive oil for sautéing

1 cup chopped onion

1 cup uncooked pearl barley

3 cups water

2 tablespoons chopped fresh basil

½ cup pomegranate seeds

½ cup shelled unsalted pistachios

This healthy and delicious grain bowl is a perfect example of simplicity with big flavors. The main goal of bowls is to eat as many colors and nutrient-dense foods as possible, so feel free to tailor your bowl to your taste preferences and get creative. For instance, top it with some Baked Kale Chips (see page 92), or switch out the barley for quick-cooking bulgur. Top it with one of the many sauces or dressings in chapter 8. Anything goes.

1. Preheat the oven to 425°F. Line a large baking sheet with parchment paper.

2. Spread the butternut squash in a single layer on the baking sheet and roast 45 to 50 minutes, stirring occasionally until it is caramelized and soft. Remove from the oven and set aside.

3. While the squash is roasting, in a medium saucepan over medium heat, heat the broth or oil for sautéing. Add the onion and cook until soft and translucent, 4 to 5 minutes. Add the barley and water and bring to a boil. Reduce the heat to a simmer and cook for 50 minutes to 1 hour, or until the grain is cooked through and all the water is absorbed. Add a little more water if it needs additional cooking time.

4. In a large bowl, combine the cooked barley, basil, cooked butternut squash, pomegranate seeds, and pistachios. Toss to combine.

Substitution Tip: If you substitute bulgur for barley, combine 1 cup bulgur with 1½ cups water and cook over low heat until tender, about 12 minutes. Remove from the heat and let stand, covered, about 10 minutes.

Per serving: Calories: 325; Fat: 3g; Saturated fat: 0g; Carbohydrate: 72g; Fiber: 14g; Sugar: 8g; Protein: 9g; Iron: 3mg; Sodium: 41mg

Toasted Barley Risotto with Savory Spinach Sauce

Serves 4 / Prep time: 20 minutes / Cook time: 1 hour

NUT-FREE, SOY-FREE

2 cups uncooked
   pearl barley

⅓ cup low-sodium
   vegetable broth
   or 2 teaspoons
   extra-virgin olive oil
   for sautéing

1½ cups chopped onion

¼ teaspoon salt

¼ teaspoon freshly
   ground black pepper

4 garlic cloves,
   chopped, divided

1 teaspoon dried basil

3 to 4 cups low-sodium
   vegetable broth

3 tablespoons fresh
   lemon juice, divided

6 cups spinach (about
   2 bunches)

Salt

Freshly ground
   black pepper

½ cup nutritional yeast

2 teaspoons freshly
   grated lemon zest

Barley has become one of my favorite plant-based grains. It has a delicious nutty flavor and a chewy, pasta-like consistency. It is also an excellent healthy replacement for traditional white arborio rice in risotto because it mimics the creaminess and richness. Of course, you can make this dish with arborio rice if you prefer.

1. Preheat the oven to 350°F. Spread the barley on a baking sheet and toast for 10 minutes. Remove and set aside.

2. In a large saucepan over medium heat, heat the broth or oil for sautéing. Add onion, salt, and pepper and cook, stirring often, until the onion is soft and translucent, 3 to 4 minutes. Add 1 chopped garlic clove. Cook for another minute. If the onion is sticking, add a little more vegetable broth.

3. Add the roasted barley, basil, and 3 cups of vegetable broth and bring to a boil. Reduce the heat and simmer, covered, stirring often, until the broth is almost absorbed. When the broth is absorbed, check for doneness. If needed, add another ¼ cup to ½ cup broth until the barley is cooked but still has a little bite and the mixture is creamy. This could

take 40 to 50 minutes. Stir frequently. When done, stir in 1 tablespoon of lemon juice and leave covered.

4. In a large saucepan, bring 2 cups of salted water to a boil. Add the spinach and cook until the leaves are bright green and wilted, about 1 minute. Drain well.

5. In a food processor, add the spinach, 2 tablespoons of vegetable broth, 1 chopped garlic clove, and the remaining 2 tablespoons of lemon juice. Purée until smooth, adding more vegetable broth if needed, until it reaches the desired consistency. Season with salt and pepper and add the nutritional yeast. Combine.

6. Add the spinach purée to the barley mixture. Season with more salt and pepper, if needed. Garnish with the lemon zest.

Serving Suggestion: Make a vegan Parmesan cheese by grinding ¼ cup pine nuts. Serve on the side.

Per serving: Calories: 529; Fat: 4g; Saturated fat: 0g; Carbohydrate: 102g; Fiber: 26g; Sugar: 5g; Protein: 28g; Iron: 5mg; Sodium: 347mg

Zoodles with Roasted Cherry Tomatoes and Basil Pesto

Serves 4 / Prep time: **15 minutes** / Cook time: **20 minutes**

GLUTEN-FREE, OIL-FREE, SOY-FREE

4 cups cherry tomatoes

¼ **teaspoon salt**

¼ **teaspoon freshly ground black pepper**

6 to 7 large zucchini

1 cup low-sodium vegetable broth, divided

2 garlic cloves, minced

6 cups stemmed, chopped kale

1 cup chopped fresh basil

¼ cup pine nuts

Simple and delicious, these zucchini noodles (known as zoodles) are paired with intensely flavored sweet roasted tomatoes and basil pesto. Zoodles are a playful way to include more vegetables and less white pasta into your diet. To make them, cut off the ends of the washed and dried unpeeled zucchini. Hold the zucchini lengthwise in your hand—kind of nested in the palm. Rest the peeler against the top edge and draw down. After you do some pulls on one side, flip it around and do the other side. Then do all sides. When you get down to the seeds, stop; you are done. The seeds don't make good zoodles.

1. Preheat the oven to 400°F.

2. Place the tomatoes on a large rimmed baking sheet. Season with the salt and pepper. Bake for 20 minutes, or until they're blistered and ready to pop open.

3. Meanwhile, make your zoodles. Place them in a wire colander and sprinkle with salt.

4. In a large skillet over medium heat, heat ½ cup of vegetable broth. Add the garlic and cook for 1 minute. Add the kale, cover the pan, and cook for 3 minutes.

5. Meanwhile, place the basil and pine nuts in a food processor with a pinch salt and pepper. Add the remaining ½ cup vegetable broth. Process until smooth, adding more vegetable broth if needed for consistency. You want it to be thin enough to toss with the zoodles.

6. Place the zoodles in a large bowl. Combine with the basil sauce. Toss with the kale and top with the roasted cherry tomatoes.

Tool Tip: I highly recommend an inexpensive julienne peeler for the perfect size zoodle.

Per serving: Calories: 237; Fat: 7g; Saturated fat: 1g; Carbohydrate: 39g; Fiber: 10g; Sugar: 15g; Protein: 13g; Iron: 5mg; Sodium: 274mg

Jen's Cannellini Meatballs with Sundried Tomatoes

Serves 4 / Prep time: 20 minutes / Cook time: 30 minutes

NUT-FREE, SOY-FREE

⅓ **cup low-sodium vegetable broth or 2 teaspoons extra-virgin olive oil for sautéing**

½ **cup chopped onion**

3 garlic cloves, chopped

1 cup canned cannellini beans, drained and rinsed, aquafaba liquid reserved (see Ingredient Tip)

1 cup cooked farro

¼ **cup chopped fresh basil, or more**

8 sundried tomatoes in oil, drained and coarsely chopped

½ **teaspoon salt**

Freshly ground black pepper

½ **cup breadcrumbs**

This comforting recipe idea is from my Italian girlfriend Jen Polenzani. It's moist, tasty, and a fun alternative to traditional Italian meatballs. I like to serve them over spaghetti squash with a little Sunday Gravy with Tomatoes and Carrots (see page 166) or Rich and Savory Mushroom Gravy (see page 164). Serve with a side of leafy greens for an extra dose of antioxidants.

1. Preheat the oven to 375°F. Line a large baking sheet with parchment paper.

2. In a medium sauté pan over medium heat, heat the broth or oil for sautéing. Add the onion and sauté until soft and translucent, 4 to 5 minutes. Add the garlic and cook for another minute.

3. Add the cannellini beans, 2 tablespoons of the aquafaba, farro, basil, onion-garlic mixture, tomatoes, salt, and pepper to a food processor. Pulse a few times until combined. Add the breadcrumbs and pulse a few more times. (I like it to have a little texture.) Taste and adjust the seasoning if needed. Add another tablespoon aquafaba if you need it to bind more.

4. Scoop out about 2 tablespoons of the mixture and gently form a small ball about 1½ inches in diameter. Place on the baking sheet. Repeat until you have used up the mixture. You will have 10 to 12 meatballs.

5. Bake for 25 minutes, until browned and firm.

Ingredient Tip: Aquafaba is the liquid in which chickpeas have been cooked. The starchy liquid, directly from the can, is a great binder. Aquafaba's other magical quality is its ability to whip to a stiff, fluffy foam, like egg whites, and create meringues. You can also use 2 flax eggs instead.

Per serving: Calories: 223; Fat: 4g; Saturated fat: 0g; Carbohydrate: 25g; Fiber: 6g; Sugar: 2g; Protein: 9g; Iron: 3mg; Sodium: 387mg

Hemp Seeds, Cannellini, and Greens

Serves 4 / Prep time: **5 minutes** / Cook time: **15 minutes**

GLUTEN-FREE, NUT-FREE, OIL-FREE, SOY-FREE

2 (15.5-ounce) cans
cannellini beans,
drained and
rinsed, aquafaba
liquid reserved

6 tablespoons hemp
seeds, divided

½ **cup low-sodium
vegetable broth, plus
¼ cup for sautéing**

¼ **teaspoon salt**

¼ **teaspoon freshly
ground black pepper**

3 garlic cloves, chopped

4 cups chopped
fresh spinach

Juice of 2 lemons

1 lemon, cut into
4 wedges

Plant-based, simple, hearty, and satisfying—what more could you ask for in a meal? It also includes one of my favorite ingredients, hemp seeds, which add a nutritional and delicious wallop to this dish. I always say if you need to run up a mountain, eat 2 tablespoons of hemp seeds for fuel. They are exceptionally rich in two essential fatty acids, omega-6 and omega-3, which provides the perfect protein and the energy to tackle anything.

1. Place the beans on a large plate or bowl and smash half the beans and 4 tablespoons of hemp seeds with a potato masher.

2. In a large sauté pan over medium heat, heat the broth for sautéing. Sprinkle with salt and pepper. Add the garlic and cook for 1 to 2 minutes or just enough for the aroma to shine through and the garlic to soften, being sure not to brown the garlic.

3. Add the smashed cannellini beans and 1 tablespoon of the bean liquid and cook for another minute. Add the greens and ½ cup of vegetable broth. Cover and cook for about 3 minutes or until the greens have softened a bit but are still shiny and green. Squeeze the lemon juice on top. Toss.

4. Garnish with the remaining 2 tablespoons of hemp seeds. Serve with lemon wedges.

Substitution Tip: Use any hearty beans, such as white, navy, or red beans, and any greens you like.

Per serving: Calories: 313; Fat: 11g; Saturated fat: 1g; Carbohydrate: 34g; Fiber: 11g; Sugar: 1g; Protein: 21g; Iron: 8mg; Sodium: 188mg

Southwestern Stuffed Peppers

Serves 4 / Prep time: 30 minutes / Cook time: 1 hour 20 minutes

GLUTEN-FREE, NUT-FREE, SOY-FREE

⅓ cup low-sodium
   vegetable broth
   or 2 teaspoons
   extra-virgin olive oil
   for sautéing

1 cup chopped onion

3 garlic cloves, chopped

1 cup uncooked wild rice

1½ cups water

4 large red or yellow
   bell peppers

1 cup frozen
   corn, thawed

1 cup cooked
   black beans

½ teaspoon salt

Freshly ground
   black pepper

1 (14.5-ounce) can diced
   tomatoes with green
   chiles, divided

Classic Southwestern ingredients stuffed into roasted peppers make a healthy, hearty entrée. It's also a good way to use leftover grains like rice. You can switch up the flavor profile by using different spices, such as ginger and soy sauce. Serve with a puddle of my Smoky Rich Cheese Sauce (see page 162).

1. Preheat the oven to 375°F.

2. In a medium saucepan over medium heat, heat the broth or oil for sautéing. Add the onion and cook until soft and translucent, 4 to 5 minutes. Add the garlic and cook 1 minute more. Add the rice and water. Bring to a boil, then cover and simmer for 30 minutes or until the rice is al dente, adding more water if needed.

3. Meanwhile, prepare the bell peppers by cutting off the tops and scooping out the seeds and as much of the membranes as you can. Set aside.

4. Put the cooked rice in a large bowl. Add the corn, black beans, salt, pepper, and 1½ cups of the diced tomatoes and combine.

5. In the bottom of a medium baking dish, spread the remaining tomatoes. Stand up the peppers in the baking dish and fill them with the rice mixture. Put the tops back on. Cover with foil and bake for 40 minutes. Remove the foil and bake for another 10 minutes.

Substitution Tip: Substitute poblano peppers for the bell peppers for a rich, earthy flavor.

Per serving: Calories: 308; Fat: 2g; Saturated fat: 0g; Carbohydrate: 65g; Fiber: 11g; Sugar: 13g; Protein: 14g; Iron: 4mg; Sodium: 523mg

Long Life Stuffed Sweet Potatoes with Black Lentils

Serves 4 / Prep time: **10 minutes** / Cook time: **50 minutes**

GLUTEN-FREE, NUT-FREE

4 large sweet potatoes

¼ cup gluten-free soy sauce

2 tablespoons pure maple syrup

⅓ **cup vegetable broth or 2 teaspoons extra-virgin olive oil for sautéing**

¾ **cup chopped onion**

2 garlic cloves

1 (1-inch) piece fresh ginger, minced

1½ cups uncooked black beluga lentils

3 to 4 cups water, divided

Freshly ground black pepper

I named this dish Long Life because people from Okinawa have a life expectancy among the highest in the world and more than 25 percent of their diet consists of sweet potatoes. And that isn't the only reason to enjoy this recipe. The earthy lentils and Asian flavors of soy and ginger give the roasted sweet potatoes a big flavor boost and perfectly complement one another. If you would like to add more vegetables, I recommend some bold, crispy Asian vegetables such as steamed Chinese cabbage or daikon.

1. Preheat the oven to 425°F. Line a large baking sheet with parchment paper.

2. Prick the sweet potatoes all over with a fork and bake until tender, or until a fork inserted into the thickest part has no resistance, 45 to 50 minutes.

3. In a small bowl, whisk together the soy sauce and maple syrup. Set aside.

4. While the sweet potatoes are cooking, in a large saucepan over medium heat, heat the broth or oil for sautéing. Add the onion and cook until soft and translucent, 3 to 4 minutes. Add the garlic and ginger and cook for another minute.

5. Add the lentils, soy sauce mixture, and 2½ cups of water. Bring to a boil and then lower to a low simmer. Cover and continue to cook over low heat, stirring occasionally and adding more water if they start to look dry, until the lentils are tender but not mushy. This should take about 25 minutes. Season with pepper.

6. Slice open the baked sweet potatoes lengthwise, top with the cooked lentils, and serve.

Serving Suggestion: Top with thinly sliced scallions and some Cashew Sour Cream (see page 151).

Per serving: Calories: 415; Fat: 1g; Saturated fat: 0g; Carbohydrate: 80g; Fiber: 27g; Sugar: 14g; Protein: 22g; Iron: 7mg; Sodium: 669mg

CHAPTER 8

Staples and Sauces

← —— Budget-Friendly Fresh Basil Pesto, p.160

Tofu Mayonnaise

Makes 1 cup / Prep time: 10 minutes

GLUTEN-FREE, NUT-FREE, OIL-FREE

1 cup silken tofu

1 tablespoon minced
   shallots

1 tablespoon Dijon
   mustard

2 tablespoons apple
   cider vinegar

⅛ cup water

Freshly ground
   black pepper

This savory, thick, creamy spread is a perfect addition to sandwiches or as a dipping sauce. This egg-free mayonnaise can be flavored in all the ways you flavor regular mayonnaise. Tofu is a wonderful source of protein and contains all nine essential amino acids that our bodies cannot produce. It's also a valuable plant source of vitamins and minerals.

In a blender or food processor, combine all the ingredients. Process until smooth and creamy.

Leftovers: Keep this in a covered jar in the refrigerator for 3 to 4 days.

Per serving (2 tablespoons): Calories: 23; Fat: 1g; Saturated fat: 0g; Carbohydrate: 1g; Fiber: 0g; Sugar: 1g; Protein: 2g; Iron: 0mg; Sodium: 34mg

Cashew Sour Cream

Makes 1 cup / Prep time: 10 minutes, plus overnight to soak

GLUTEN-FREE, OIL-FREE, SOY-FREE

1 cup raw unsalted
   cashews

1 tablespoon fresh
   lemon juice

1½ tablespoons apple
   cider vinegar

¼ teaspoon salt

Freshly ground
   black pepper

This rich and tangy vegan sour cream is the perfect accompaniment to baked sweet potatoes or vegetables, or dolloped on top of a stew. Add it during the last 5 minutes of cooking soups to thicken and intensify flavors. If you don't want to use nuts as the base, substitute a cup of silken tofu and use the same ingredients. Both flavor and texture are close to the dairy version.

1. Place the cashews in a bowl and cover with water. Let soak for at least 2 hours, or overnight.

2. Drain and rinse the cashews. Add all the ingredients to a food processor and process until they're thick and creamy, adding a little water if needed.

Leftovers: Store covered in the refrigerator for 3 days.

Per serving (2 tablespoons): Calories: 87; Fat: 7g; Saturated fat: 1g; Carbohydrate: 5g; Fiber: 1g; Sugar: 1g; Protein: 2g; Iron: 1mg; Sodium: 77mg

No-Nut Butter

Makes 2 cups / Prep time: 10 minutes

GLUTEN-FREE, NUT-FREE, SOY-FREE

1½ cups unsalted shelled sunflower seeds

½ cup ground flaxseed

¼ cup sesame seeds

½ cup sunflower oil

2 tablespoons pure maple syrup

2 tablespoons water

½ teaspoon salt

Peanut allergy is the second-most-common food allergy in children and seems to be on the rise. Here's a creamy, nutty butter that is allergen-free. Use it in place of peanut butter on toast or in recipes. Sunflower seeds are less pricey than most seeds, but you can also add or substitute hemp or chia seeds. This seed butter will keep in the refrigerator in a sealed container up to 2 weeks.

1. In a food processor, add all the ingredients. Process until smooth.

2. If the consistency is too thick, add a little more water.

Tool Tip: A high-speed food processor or blender is one of the best investments you can make; healthy eating is much easier with the right appliances.

Per serving (1 tablespoon): Calories: 84; Fat: 8g; Saturated fat: 1g; Carbohydrate: 3g; Fiber: 2g; Sugar: 1g; Protein: 2g; Iron: 1mg; Sodium: 35mg

Oil-Free Pinto Bean Dressing

Makes 1 cup / Prep time: 10 minutes

GLUTEN-FREE, NUT-FREE, OIL-FREE, SOY-FREE

¼ cup plus
  2 tablespoons cooked
  pinto beans

1½ teaspoons Dijon
  mustard

1 tablespoon apple
  cider vinegar

1½ teaspoons minced
  shallots

2 tablespoons chopped
  fresh parsley

¼ teaspoon freshly
  ground black pepper

I love oil-free salad dressings. There is no nutritional value in most oils; vegetable oils contain no fiber or minerals and are 100 percent fat calories. When it comes to building dressings, you can adapt some of your favorite flavors without the use of oils. A simple combination of a whole-food fat like avocado, an acid like vinegar, a sweet element like maple syrup, and fresh herbs can create delicious flavor profiles. The pinto beans add a creamy texture and smoky flavor to this salad dressing. Don't hesitate to experiment.

1. In a food processor, add the beans, mustard, vinegar, and shallots. Process until smooth.

2. Add the parsley and pepper and pulse to lightly combine. If the dressing is too thick, add a little water.

Leftovers: This will keep, covered, in the refrigerator for 3 to 5 days.

Per serving (2 tablespoons): Calories: 8; Fat: 0g; Saturated fat: 0g; Carbohydrate: 1g; Fiber: 0g; Sugar: 0g; Protein: 1g; Iron: 0mg; Sodium: 11mg

Citrus Tahini Dressing

Makes 1 cup / Prep time: 5 minutes

GLUTEN-FREE, NUT-FREE, SOY-FREE

½ cup orange juice

⅓ cup tahini

2 tablespoons apple cider vinegar

1 tablespoon pure maple syrup

¼ cup chopped fresh cilantro (optional)

2 tablespoons extra-virgin olive oil

1 garlic clove, minced

Freshly ground black pepper

¼ teaspoon salt

This dressing is tangy, creamy, sweet, and tastes delicious over hearty greens like kale or roasted beets. Tahini has the same earthy, nutty flavor as sesame seeds because it's made from ground sesame. If you are not a fan of cilantro, substitute parsley. And try fresh blood orange juice instead of orange juice for a deeper flavor.

1. In a food processor, add all the ingredients. Process until smooth.

2. Taste and adjust the seasoning.

Leftovers: This will last covered in the refrigerator for up to 3 days.

Per serving (2 tablespoons): Calories: 93; Fat: 8g; Saturated fat: 1g; Carbohydrate: 5g; Fiber: 1g; Sugar: 3g; Protein: 2g; Iron: 1mg; Sodium: 77mg

Thai Flavor Bomb

Makes about 16 cubes / Prep time: 5 minutes

GLUTEN-FREE, NUT-FREE, OIL-FREE

1½ cups fresh Thai or regular basil

½ cup light coconut milk

3 tablespoons fresh lime juice

1½ tablespoons minced fresh ginger

2 tablespoons gluten-free soy sauce

Freshly ground black pepper

Flavor bombs are blends of savory ingredients and fresh herbs that you can make in advance and freeze in ice cube trays. Just drop them frozen into stir-fries, rice and other grains, soups, and stews. If you like heat, add a couple of chopped red or green Fresno chiles.

1. In a food processor, add all the ingredients. Process until smooth.

2. Spoon the flavor bombs into ice cube trays and freeze. Once frozen, transfer the cubes to an airtight container or a resealable freezer bag.

Leftovers: These flavor bombs will keep in the freezer for 2 months. When you're preparing a stir-fry, soup, or stew, throw 2 or 3 into the heated pan. You can also use up any leftover herbs this way. Just combine the herbs with some vegetable broth and freeze.

Per serving (1 cube): Calories: 22; Fat: 2g; Saturated fat: 2g; Carbohydrate: 2g; Fiber: 0g; Sugar: 0g; Protein: 0g; Iron: 0mg; Sodium: 114mg

Sweet and Spicy Peanut Sauce

Makes ½ cup / Prep time: 5 minutes

GLUTEN-FREE, OIL-FREE

1 garlic clove, chopped

⅓ cup peanut butter

2 tablespoons gluten-free soy sauce or tamari

1 tablespoon pure maple syrup

2 tablespoons fresh lime juice

1 teaspoon sriracha sauce, or more to taste

⅛ cup water

This creamy and savory peanut sauce can be whipped up in an instant and makes a great addition to Asian-inspired noodles, salads, and spring rolls, like my Crunchy Vegetable Spring Rolls (see page 98). It's one sauce with endless possibilities. Peanuts are also an especially good source of healthy fats, protein, and fiber. Although it's true that there are numerous health benefits to peanut butter, not all peanut butter brands use the healthiest ingredients. Check the label and make sure the peanut butter contains just one or two ingredients.

1. In a food processor or high-speed blender, combine all the ingredients.

2. Process until smooth, adding more water for a thinner consistency.

Substitution Tip: If you have allergies, use No-Nut Butter (see page 152) in place of the peanut butter.

Per serving (2 tablespoons): Calories: 147; Fat: 11g; Saturated fat: 2g; Carbohydrate: 9g; Fiber: 1g; Sugar: 5g; Protein: 6g; Iron: 2mg; Sodium: 551mg

Pear Chutney

Makes 2 cups / Prep time: **10 minutes** / Cook time: **45 minutes**

GLUTEN-FREE, NUT-FREE, OIL-FREE, SOY-FREE

1¾ pounds fresh pears, peeled, cored, and chopped

2 tablespoons chopped shallots

½ cup rice wine vinegar

2 tablespoons pure maple syrup

½ cup golden raisins

½ teaspoon salt

Freshly ground black pepper

Delight your taste buds with this flavorful pear condiment. For best results, use Bosc, d'Anjou, or Bartlett pears that are firm and slightly underripe. You can also make this recipe with apples instead of pears, or a combination of the two. Pears are one of nature's healthiest fruits. They are rich in important antioxidants, flavonoids, and dietary fiber. Consuming fruits of all kinds has long been associated with a reduced risk of a range of health conditions. This chutney tastes delicious with Samosa Patties (see page 126).

1. In a medium saucepan over medium-high heat, combine all the ingredients. Bring to a boil and reduce the heat to a simmer.

2. Cook uncovered for 40 to 45 minutes, stirring occasionally, until thickened. Serve warm or chilled.

Leftovers: Store in the refrigerator in an airtight container for up to 1 week.

Per serving (2 tablespoons): Calories: 55; Fat: 0g; Saturated fat: 0g; Carbohydrate: 13g; Fiber: 2g; Sugar: 9g; Protein: 0g; Iron: 0mg; Sodium: 75mg

Roasted Tomatillo Salsa

Makes 2 cups / Prep time: 5 minutes / Cook time: 30 minutes

GLUTEN-FREE, NUT-FREE, OIL-FREE, SOY-FREE

3 tomatillos, husked
and halved

1 Anaheim chile, seeded
and chopped

1 jalapeño pepper,
seeded and chopped

2 plum tomatoes,
quartered

**2 garlic cloves, whole in
their skin**

**½ onion, coarsely
chopped**

1 tablespoon fresh
lime juice

¼ teaspoon salt

**¼ teaspoon freshly
ground black pepper**

Kick your salsa up a notch. Roasting peppers brings out delicious, fresh, smoky, complex flavors. Studies have suggested that the capsaicin in peppers boosts metabolism, which can help burn calories. If you like heat, add one more jalapeño pepper—but taste before you add it! You can also substitute poblano peppers for the tomatillos. This unique salsa is perfect for tacos, on top of a stir-fry, or on a simple baked sweet potato. Or try it on top of my Black Bean Burgers with Quinoa Breadcrumbs (see page 86).

1. Preheat the oven to 400°F.

2. On a large baking sheet, arrange the tomatillos, Anaheim chile, jalapeño pepper, tomatoes, garlic, and onion in a single layer and roast until the vegetables are softened and slightly caramelized, 25 to 30 minutes.

3. Squeeze the roasted cloves of garlic out of their skin. Transfer all the roasted vegetables to a food processor or blender. Add the lime juice, and process until combined, but still chunky, about 10 seconds. Add the salt and pepper.

Ingredient Tip: Tomatillos are fruits native to Mexico, with a flavor similar to tomatoes but more acidic and fruity. Look for tomatillos with dry husks that tightly cover the fruit. Remove the papery husk with your hands and discard, and then rinse off the sticky residue it leaves behind. The fruit should be firm without much give and no dark or soft spots.

Per serving: Calories: 17; Fat: 0g; Saturated fat: 0g; Carbohydrate: 4g; Fiber: 1g; Sugar: 2g; Protein: 1g; Iron: 0mg; Sodium: 78mg

Budget-Friendly Fresh Basil Pesto

Makes 1 cup / Prep time: **5 minutes**

GLUTEN-FREE, OIL-FREE, SOY-FREE

3 tablespoons pine nuts

2 teaspoons minced garlic

¾ cup plain vegan yogurt

2 tablespoons nutritional yeast

2 tablespoons fresh lemon juice

¼ teaspoon salt

Freshly ground black pepper

1½ cups loosely packed fresh basil

In my search for a pine nut pesto that will not break the bank, I developed this creamy, zesty, healthy, satisfying vegan pesto. Unfortunately, pine nuts can be expensive, but there is a reason for that. They come from pine cones and are nestled in between the cone scales. It is long and tedious work to extract these sweet nuts. This recipe still provides the rich and creamy taste of pine nuts but saves money by using plain unflavored vegan yogurt as a base. You can also use soft tofu as the base.

1. Place the pine nuts in a dry frying pan large enough to hold them in a single layer. Turn the heat to medium-low and cook until they're fragrant and golden brown, shaking to keeping them moving to prevent sticking or burning. The toasting will only take 2 or 3 minutes, so don't leave them unattended.

2. In a food processor, combine the toasted pine nuts, garlic, yogurt, nutritional yeast, lemon juice, salt, and pepper. Process until smooth.

3. Add the basil and pulse just to break up the leaves.

Serving Suggestion: This fresh pesto is not only perfect for pasta, but you can also use it as a dip, in wraps, on sandwiches and salads, tossed with zoodles, or dolloped on Buddha bowls. Don't be afraid to get creative with your pesto.

Per serving (2 tablespoons): Calories: 56; Fat: 3g; Saturated fat: 0g; Carbohydrate: 4g; Fiber: 1g; Sugar: 1g; Protein: 3g; Iron: 1mg; Sodium: 77mg

Smoky Rich Cheese Sauce

Makes 2 cups / Prep time: 10 minutes, plus overnight to soak

GLUTEN-FREE, OIL-FREE, SOY-FREE

1 cup unsalted raw
cashews, soaked in
water overnight or
for at least 2 hours
and drained

3 tablespoons fresh
lemon juice

½ cup roasted
red or yellow
pepper, chopped

1½ teaspoons
onion powder

⅓ cup nutritional yeast

1 cup water

This silky smooth sauce is ideal for pasta or poured over vegetables like steamed broccoli and baked potatoes. I often toss it with pasta and top with crispy breadcrumbs for a super-satisfying quick vegan mac and cheese. No matter how you use it, this creamy, cheesy sauce is delicious. Plus, cashews contain heart-healthy monounsaturated fats, including oleic and palmitoleic acids, essential fatty acids associated with lower levels of unhealthy LDL cholesterol and higher levels of healthy HDL cholesterol.

In a food processor or high-speed blender, combine all the ingredients. Blend until smooth.

Preparation Tip: To soak your cashews, place them in a bowl and cover with water by an inch, then cover and soak at room temperature up to 4 hours. Longer than 4 hours, put them in the refrigerator to soak overnight. Don't soak longer than overnight, because oversoaking cashews can make them bitter.

Per serving (¼ cup): Calories: 136; Fat: 7g; Saturated fat: 1g; Carbohydrate: 11g; Fiber: 4g; Sugar: 1g; Protein: 9g; Iron: 2mg; Sodium: 6mg

Creamy Smoky Chipotle Sauce

Makes 1½ cups / Prep time: 5 minutes

GLUTEN-FREE, NUT-FREE, OIL-FREE

3 to 5 whole chipotles in adobo sauce, chopped

4 garlic cloves, chopped

1½ cups soft tofu

¼ cup fresh lime juice

2½ tablespoons pure maple syrup

Salt

Freshly ground black pepper

This easy, creamy sauce with just the right amount of spice is a wonderful condiment to keep on hand. Use it to spice up your favorite tacos, vegetables, and bowls. Or use it as a dip for sweet potato fries. Chipotle is a smoked hot chile used in Mexican cooking, so this sauce can accompany any Mexican-inspired dishes, such as nachos, tostadas, or enchiladas. Chipotle peppers are low in fat and calories and contain a compound called capsaicin, which increases metabolism.

1. Add all the ingredients to a food processor, beginning with 2 or 3 chopped chipotles. Process until smooth.

2. Taste and season with more chipotles if needed, and salt and pepper. Process again until smooth.

Leftovers: After opening the can of chipotle peppers, transfer any leftovers to a resealable jar and keep in the refrigerator for up to 1 month. Or blend any leftovers into a smooth paste and freeze in ice cube trays. Smoky, spicy chipotle peppers can add a boost to soups, chili, hummus, black beans, or just about anything.

Per serving (¼ cup): Calories: 72; Fat: 3g; Saturated fat: 0g; Carbohydrate: 9g; Fiber: 1g; Sugar: 6g; Protein: 5g; Iron: 2mg; Sodium: 196mg

Rich and Savory Mushroom Gravy

Makes 3 cups / Prep time: 10 minutes / Cook time: 30 minutes

GLUTEN-FREE, NUT-FREE, SOY-FREE

3 tablespoons reduced-sodium tamari

3 tablespoons nutritional yeast

2 tablespoons rice flour

⅓ cup low-sodium vegetable broth or 2 teaspoons extra-virgin olive oil for sautéing

1 onion, chopped

3 cups mushrooms, chopped

4 garlic cloves, chopped

1 tablespoon chopped fresh thyme

2½ cups low-sodium vegetable broth

This gravy is super-rich and beautifully flavored; no one will believe it's vegan! Don't save this recipe just for the holidays. Use it any time of year ladled over potatoes, vegetables, and many of the recipes in this book—including Jen's Cannellini Meatballs with Sundried Tomatoes (see page 140) and Grilled Portobello Mushrooms over Cauliflower Mash (see page 124).

1. In a small bowl, whisk together the tamari, nutritional yeast, and flour to form a thick paste. Set aside.

2. In a large sauté pan over medium heat, heat the broth or oil for sautéing. Add the onion and mushrooms and sauté until the vegetables are soft, 4 to 5 minutes. Add the garlic and thyme and cook 1 minute more. Stir in the 2½ cups vegetable broth. Bring to a boil, reduce the heat, and simmer for 20 minutes.

3. Add the tamari paste, whisking constantly to make sure it dissolves. Bring to a boil, lower to a simmer, and cook for 5 minutes or more, adding more broth if needed. If you prefer the gravy thicker, whisk in another tablespoon of flour.

4. Let it cool and put in a food processor or blender. Process until smooth.

5. Reheat to serve.

Substitution Tip: Use portobello, cremini, or white mushrooms or a combination. And 2 tablespoons of chopped fresh sage for a more traditional holiday gravy.

Per serving (¼ cup): Calories: 37; Fat: 0g; Saturated fat: 0g; Carbohydrate: 6g; Fiber: 2g; Sugar: 1g; Protein: 4g; Iron: 1mg; Sodium: 193mg

Sunday Gravy with Tomatoes and Carrots

Makes 6 cups / Prep time: **10 minutes** / Cook time: **30 minutes**

GLUTEN-FREE, NUT-FREE, SOY-FREE

⅓ cup vegetable broth or 2 teaspoons extra-virgin olive oil for sautéing

½ cup diced white onion

3 garlic cloves, minced

5 cups tomatoes, fresh or canned, cored and diced small

1 carrot, finely grated

Salt

Freshly ground black pepper

Take your taste buds on an Italian vacation with this fresh, quick, easy tomato-based sauce that has a touch of sweetness from the carrot. Don't just save it for pasta; serve it over grilled vegetables, zoodles, or roasted spaghetti squash. Use as a sauce for Jen's Cannellini Meatballs with Sundried Tomatoes (see page 140) or Italian-Style Spaghetti Squash (see page 109).

1. In a large sauté pan over medium heat, heat the broth or oil for sautéing. Sauté the onion until soft and translucent, 4 to 5 minutes. Add the garlic and cook another minute.

2. Add the tomatoes and carrot and cook on medium-low for about 25 minutes, stirring occasionally.

3. Let cool and transfer to a food processor. Process until everything is smooth and combined.

4. Season with salt and pepper.

Preparation Tip: Add one more finely grated carrot for extra sweetness.

Per serving (¼ cup): Calories: 45; Fat: 0g; Saturated fat: 0g; Carbohydrate: 7g; Fiber: 0g; Sugar: 6g; Protein: 4g; Iron: 0mg; Sodium: 82mg

Cashew Béchamel White Sauce

Makes 3½ to 4 cups / Prep time: **10 minutes, plus overnight to soak** / Cook time: **5 minutes**

GLUTEN-FREE, SOY-FREE

2 cups raw unsalted cashews

⅓ cup vegetable broth or 2 teaspoons extra-virgin olive oil for sautéing

1 cup diced onion

2 garlic cloves, diced

1½ cups vegetable broth

½ cup dry white wine

2½ tablespoons nutritional yeast

Pinch nutmeg

1 teaspoon salt

Freshly ground black pepper

Every cook needs a good, simple white sauce in their repertoire because it can be used in many ways. I like this béchamel over homemade pizza with mushrooms and spinach, in lasagna, or as a thickener. You can also ladle it over steamed vegetables for a creamy side dish. Dishes that are scalloped or baked au gratin are often made with white sauces as a base, often topped with breadcrumbs.

1. In a medium bowl, cover the cashews in water. Let sit for at least 2 hours or overnight to soften. Drain and rinse.

2. In a medium sauté pan over medium heat, heat the broth or oil for sautéing. Add the onion and cook until soft and translucent, 4 to 5 minutes. Add the garlic and cook for 1 minute more.

3. Place the onion mixture into a food processor. Add the cashews, 1½ cups vegetable broth, white wine, nutritional yeast, nutmeg, salt, and pepper. Process until smooth. Add more liquid for a thinner consistency.

Per serving (¼ cup): Calories: 123; Fat: 8g; Saturated fat: 1g; Carbohydrate: 8g; Fiber: 2g; Sugar: 2g; Protein: 5g; Iron: 1mg; Sodium: 250mg

OV Community Hollandaise Sauce

Makes 1 cup / Prep time: 10 minutes / Cook time: 30 minutes

GLUTEN-FREE, OIL-FREE, SOY-FREE

2 cups fresh or frozen and thawed corn kernels (from about 4 small ears)

¼ teaspoon salt, plus a pinch, divided

1½ cups unsweetened almond milk

½ teaspoon ground turmeric

2 to 2½ tablespoons fresh lemon juice

¼ teaspoon cayenne pepper

Freshly ground black pepper

When I asked our health and wellness community on Facebook which vegan sauce they would like me to include in this cookbook, the consensus was hollandaise. Most vegan hollandaise sauce recipes call for cashews as the base, and I wanted to try something different but with a similar flavor. I discovered it in the juice of corn kernels. This low-fat, plant-based version has many of the same savory flavors as traditional egg-and-butter-based hollandaise, but it's much lighter. If you want your sauce to be thicker, whisk in a little tapioca or cornstarch when reheating it in a saucepan.

1. Preheat the oven to 375°F. Line a large baking sheet with parchment paper.

2. Spread the corn kernels on the baking sheet in a single even layer. Sprinkle with a pinch salt. Roast for 30 minutes or until the corn is crisp and begins to brown.

3. In a food processor, add the roasted corn, almond milk, turmeric, and salt and purée for 2 to 3 minutes. Remove from the food processor and press the corn purée through a fine-mesh strainer into a medium bowl, pressing the solids to extract as much liquid as possible. Discard the solids.

4. Into the extracted liquid, stir in the lemon juice, cayenne pepper, and the remaining ¼ teaspoon salt. Season with pepper and a little more lemon juice if needed.

5. Keep any leftover sauce in a sealed container in the refrigerator for 3 to 4 days.

Substitution Tip: Kala namak, also known as Himalayan black salt, will give this recipe a sulfuric "eggy" flavor. Or spike this sauce with your favorite fresh herbs. Serve over asparagus, baked tofu, or broccoli, or create a Benedict with English muffins and Portobello Bacon (see page 101).

Per serving (2 tablespoons): Calories: 50; Fat: 2g; Saturated fat: 0g; Carbohydrate: 8g; Fiber: 2g; Sugar: 1g; Protein: 2g; Iron: 1mg; Sodium: 148mg

CHAPTER 9

Sweets

← Chocolate Peanut Butter Cups, p.177

Vegan Whipped Cream

Makes 2 cups / Prep time: 10 minutes, plus overnight to chill

GLUTEN-FREE, NUT-FREE, SOY-FREE

1 (13- to 14-ounce) can unsweetened, full-fat coconut milk

3 teaspoons sugar or any vegan sweetener

1 teaspoon pure vanilla extract

This light, fluffy whipped cream turns any dessert or drink into a 10! Remember to use pure vanilla bean extract.

1. Refrigerate the can of full-fat coconut milk overnight.

2. Place a large metal bowl and electric beaters from an electric hand mixer in the freezer for 1 hour before preparing the whipped cream.

3. Open the cold can of coconut milk without shaking it. The coconut cream solids will have hardened on the top. Spoon just the solids into the cold mixing bowl, avoiding the liquid. (You can save the liquid to make smoothies, puddings, or overnight oats.)

4. Using an electric mixer with the chilled beaters, beat the coconut cream on high until stiff peaks form.

5. Add the sugar and vanilla and beat another minute. Taste and add more sweetener if needed.

Leftovers: This whipped cream will stay fresh for 3 to 5 days in a sealed container in the refrigerator.

Per serving (2 tablespoons): Calories: 41; Fat: 2g; Saturated fat: 2g; Carbohydrate: 6g; Fiber: 0g; Sugar: 6g; Protein: 0g; Iron: 0mg; Sodium: 4mg

Patty's Three-Minute Fudge

Makes 64 pieces / Prep time: 10 minutes, plus 1 hour to cool

GLUTEN-FREE, NUT-FREE, SOY-FREE

Vegan butter

2 cups dark semisweet vegan chocolate chips

1 (14.5-ounce) can vegan sweetened condensed milk

1 teaspoon vanilla extract

This recipe is dedicated to my courageous childhood friend Patty Smith, who fought breast cancer most of her life. She always made me this fudge growing up. It was our after-school treat, and often we wouldn't wait for it to cool before eating it; we would just slurp it down with a spoon. There is something about childhood memories and friends that you can never replace, but sometimes eating the food you shared together can take you right back to those special moments.

1. Grease an 8-inch square pan with vegan butter and line with parchment paper.

2. In a microwave-safe two-quart bowl, heat the chocolate chips and condensed milk on high for 1 minute. Let sit for 1 minute, then stir to combine. If needed, heat an additional 30 seconds. Stir until the chips are completely melted and the chocolate is smooth. Stir in the vanilla.

3. Pour the fudge into the prepared pan. Allow it to cool and set, about 1 hour, before cutting into squares.

4. The fudge will keep at room temperature, covered, for 1 to 2 days.

continued →

Patty's Three-Minute Fudge *continued*

Ingredient Tip: Chocolate is made from cacao, cocoa butter, sugar, and sometimes dairy products. The lower the quality, the more sugar and dairy are added. Many brands of high-quality, high-cocoa-content chocolate are vegan. Just read the labels and they won't be hard to find.

Per serving: Calories: 89; Fat: 4g; Saturated fat: 3g; Carbohydrate: 12g; Fiber: 0g; Sugar: 2g; Protein: 1g; Iron: 1mg; Sodium: 5mg

Healthy Avocado Chocolate Pudding

Serves 4 / Prep time: 5 minutes

GLUTEN-FREE, NUT-FREE, OIL-FREE, SOY-FREE

6 avocados, peeled, pitted, and cut into chunks

½ cup pure maple syrup, or more to taste

¾ cup unsweetened cocoa powder

2 teaspoons vanilla extract

Fresh mint leaves, optional

This avocado pudding is as chocolaty and luscious as any pudding you could prepare, without all the unhealthy ingredients. Avocados are a great source of vitamins C, E, K, and B6, as well as omega-3 fatty acids, magnesium, potassium, and beta carotene. These nutrients can boost heart health, improve digestion, help keep eyes healthy, and protect skin from aging. There is no doubt that this humble, beautiful fruit is one of the healthiest foods on the planet. This dessert tastes additionally yummy topped with Vegan Whipped Cream (see page 172).

1. In a food processor, purée the avocados, maple syrup, cocoa powder, and vanilla until smooth.

2. Garnish with mint leaves, if desired.

Ingredient Tip: Avoid leftovers and eat it all! The avocado will oxidize and turn brown after just a few hours.

Per serving: Calories: 578; Fat: 42g; Saturated fat: 7g; Carbohydrate: 58g; Fiber: 23g; Sugar: 25g; Protein: 8g; Iron: 4mg; Sodium: 28mg

Mexican Chocolate Mousse

Serves 4 / Prep time: 15 minutes, plus 1 hour to chill

GLUTEN-FREE, NUT-FREE, OIL-FREE

8 ounces bittersweet
or semisweet vegan
chocolate

1¾ cups (about 1 pound)
silken tofu

½ cup pure maple syrup

1 teaspoon vanilla

1½ teaspoons ground
cinnamon

This light and not-too-sweet dessert will satisfy any chocolate lover. I call this dish a mousse because the tofu gives it a light and airy texture. In colonial times, cinnamon from the Far East was introduced into Mexican cuisine, and the combination of chocolate, cinnamon, and vanilla became authentically Mexican. Later, hot peppers and unsweetened chocolate were combined in the savory sauce we now know as molé. So there is a rich history behind this Mexican chocolate dessert. I like to top it with my Vegan Whipped Cream (see page 172).

1. Create a double boiler by bringing a medium pot filled halfway with water to a low simmer. Place a heatproof bowl on top so it is not touching the water. Add the chocolate to the bowl. Keep the pot over low heat and stir the chocolate until it is melted and silky smooth.

2. In a food processor or blender, add all the ingredients. Blend until smooth.

3. Refrigerate for at least 1 hour before serving.

Substitution Tip: Substitute 1 teaspoon of chili powder for the ground cinnamon or add both for an authentic Mexican chocolate experience.

Per serving: Calories: 442; Fat: 18g; Saturated fat: 10g; Carbohydrate: 68g; Fiber: 1g; Sugar: 26g; Protein: 12g; Iron: 4mg; Sodium: 44mg

Chocolate Peanut Butter Cups

Makes 9 pieces / Prep time: 20 minutes, plus 40 minutes to chill

GLUTEN-FREE, OIL-FREE, SOY-FREE

5 ounces vegan semisweet chocolate, divided

½ cup smooth peanut butter

½ teaspoon vanilla

¼ teaspoon salt

These chocolate peanut butter cups are a chocolate lover's dream. Nutty peanut butter and rich, smooth chocolate are the perfect match. The addition of salt is the closest thing to a magic ingredient: When you add salt to chocolate, fuller, richer, and more complex flavors emerge. These can be considered a guilt-free pleasure because chocolate contains high levels of antioxidants.

1. Line a muffin tray with 9 mini or regular paper cupcake liners.

2. Place half the chocolate in a microwave-safe bowl and microwave on high for 25 seconds, then take it out and stir. Place the bowl back in the microwave and repeat the process of cooking for 25 seconds, stopping and stirring, until the chocolate has melted.

3. Spoon 1 to 1½ teaspoons of melted chocolate into each cup. Place in the refrigerator for 10 minutes until solid.

4. Meanwhile, in a medium bowl, stir together the peanut butter, vanilla, and salt. Transfer the peanut butter mixture to a resealable plastic bag and seal it tightly. Cut off one

continued →

corner of the plastic bag and squeeze the bag to pipe 2 to 3 teaspoons of peanut butter into the center of each cup. Smooth with a small spoon.

5. Melt the remaining chocolate. Spoon 1 to 1½ teaspoons of chocolate into the top of each cup. Smooth with a small spoon.

6. Refrigerate until solid, 30 to 40 minutes. Peel off the liners and enjoy. Remove from refrigerator and let sit for 15 minutes if you like a softer chocolate.

Leftovers: Store leftovers in the refrigerator up to 2 weeks or in the freezer up to 1 month.

Per serving (1 cup): Calories: 177; Fat: 13g; Saturated fat: 5g; Carbohydrate: 15g; Fiber: 1g; Sugar: 2g; Protein: 5g; Iron: 1mg; Sodium: 76mg

Banana Ice Cream with Chocolate Sauce

Serves 4 / Prep time: 10 minutes, plus 2 hours to soak or overnight to soak

GLUTEN-FREE, OIL-FREE, SOY-FREE

½ cup raw unsalted cashews

¼ cup pure maple syrup

1 tablespoon unsweetened cocoa powder

1 teaspoon vanilla extract

¼ **teaspoon salt**

¼ **cup water**

6 ripe bananas, peeled and frozen (see Ingredient Tip)

Once you taste healthy frozen banana ice cream, you will never need any other kind. You will also be surprised how quick and easy this delicious dessert is to prepare. Bananas are extremely nutritious and low in calories and fat. Consider adding ½ teaspoon of a spice like cardamom, cinnamon, or ginger. Or, for a different flavor, replace the chocolate sauce with fresh or frozen berries.

1. Place the cashews in a small bowl and cover with water. Let soak for at least 2 hours or overnight. Drain and rinse.

2. In a food processor or blender, place the cashews, maple syrup, cocoa powder, vanilla, and salt. Blend, adding the water a couple of tablespoons at a time until you get a smooth consistency.

3. Transfer to an airtight container and refrigerate until needed. Bring to room temperature before using.

4. Place the frozen bananas in a food processor. Process until you have smooth banana ice cream. Serve topped with chocolate sauce.

continued →

Banana Ice Cream with Chocolate Sauce *continued*

Ingredient Tip: The best way to freeze a banana is to start with ripe peeled bananas. Slice them into 2-inch chunks and arrange them in a single layer on a parchment-lined baking sheet. Pop them in the freezer. Once frozen, transfer to freezer-safe bags. Frozen bananas are also a delicious, healthy addition for smoothies. Individually freeze chunks of one banana and you'll always be ready to create an icy, rich, creamy smoothie.

Per serving: Calories: 301; Fat: 8g; Saturated fat: 2g; Carbohydrate: 59g; Fiber: 6g; Sugar: 34g; Protein: 5g; Iron: 2mg; Sodium: 154mg

Raspberry Lime Sorbet

Serves 4 / Prep time: 15 minutes, plus 5 hours or more to chill

GLUTEN-FREE, NUT-FREE, OIL-FREE, SOY-FREE

3 pints fresh raspberries or 2 (10-ounce) bags frozen

½ cup fresh orange juice (from 2 medium oranges)

4 tablespoons pure maple syrup

3 tablespoons fresh lime juice

Dark chocolate curls, optional

This fruity, refreshing frozen treat is simple to prepare and has incredible health benefits. One cup of raspberries provides more than 50 percent of the minimum daily target for vitamin C, which supports immunity and skin health and helps produce collagen, a structural protein. If raspberries are out of season, don't hesitate to use frozen fruit because it's packaged at the peak of ripeness.

1. In a shallow glass dish, combine the raspberries, orange juice, maple syrup, and lime juice. Stir well to mix. Cover and put in the freezer until frozen solid, about 5 hours.

2. Remove from the freezer and let it sit for 10 minutes. Break off chunks with a knife or large spoon and transfer the mixture to a food processor. Process until smooth and creamy, about 5 minutes. Serve immediately or place back into the freezer for up to 1 hour before serving. The sorbet will freeze solid again but can be processed again until creamy just before serving.

3. To serve, place a scoop into an ice cream dish. Garnish with fresh raspberries and dark chocolate curls, if using.

continued →

Raspberry Lime Sorbet *continued*

Preparation Tip: To make chocolate curls, use a vegetable peeler and scrape the blade lengthwise across a piece of solid chocolate to create pretty, delicate curls. Refrigerate the curls until ready to use.

Per serving: Calories: 191; Fat: 2g; Saturated fat: 0g; Carbohydrate: 46g; Fiber: 15g; Sugar: 25g; Protein: 3g; Iron: 2mg; Sodium: 5mg

Baked Apples with Dried Fruit

Serves 4 / Prep time: **10 minutes** / Cook time: **1 hour**

GLUTEN-FREE, NUT-FREE, OIL-FREE, SOY-FREE

- 4 large apples, cored to make a cavity
- 4 teaspoons raisins or cranberries
- 4 teaspoons pure maple syrup
- ½ teaspoon ground cinnamon
- ½ cup unsweetened apple juice or water

There is no healthier and easier dessert to prepare than baked fruit. Their juices bubble up and naturally produce a sweet, rich fruit sauce. I prefer a delicious variety of apples for this dish but use whatever you like. Pick your favorite dried fruit, too; just chop it into small pieces so it fits in the apple core.

1. Preheat the oven to 350°F.

2. Place the apples in a baking dish that will hold them upright. Put the dried fruit into the cavities and drizzle with maple syrup. Sprinkle with cinnamon. Pour the apple juice or water around the apples.

3. Cover loosely with foil and bake for 50 minutes to 1 hour, or until the apples are tender when pierced with a fork.

Serving Suggestion: Serve the apples topped with Vegan Whipped Cream (see page 172).

Per serving: Calories: 158; Fat: 1g; Saturated fat: 0g; Carbohydrate: 42g; Fiber: 6g; Sugar: 32g; Protein: 1g; Iron: 1mg; Sodium: 4mg

Hemp Seed Brittle

Serves 6 / Prep time: **10 minutes, plus time to cool** / Cook time: **10 minutes**

GLUTEN-FREE, NUT-FREE, SOY-FREE

¼ cup hemp seeds

2½ tablespoons brown rice flour

3 tablespoons melted coconut oil

2½ tablespoons pure maple syrup

Pinch salt

This quick, healthy, and guilt-free brittle is made with one of the healthiest seeds on earth. Hemp seeds are a great protein source and contain high amounts of vitamin E, calcium, iron, and zinc. The human body does not store zinc, so it is important to include zinc in your diet. You can replace some or all of the hemp seeds with shelled pumpkin seeds or sunflower seeds.

1. Preheat the oven to 350°F. Line a baking sheet with parchment paper.

2. In a medium bowl, combine all the ingredients and mix well. Spread into an even layer on the baking sheet. Try to get it as even as possible, or the edges will burn.

3. Bake for 10 minutes and watch carefully to make sure the brittle doesn't burn. Shut off the oven and leave the pan in for 30 minutes to cool down.

4. When it's completely cooled, break into bite-size pieces with a sharp knife or your fingers.

Leftovers: Store leftovers in a sealed container at room temperature for 5 days or freeze for up to 1 month.

Per serving: Calories: 151; Fat: 12g; Saturated fat: 6g; Carbohydrate: 9g; Fiber: 1g; Sugar: 5g; Protein: 4g; Iron: 1mg; Sodium: 28mg

Cardamom Date Bites

Makes 24 bites / Prep time: 15 minutes, plus time to soak / Cook time: 15 minutes
NUT-FREE, OIL-FREE, SOY-FREE

1 cup pitted dates

3 cups old-fashioned rolled oats

¼ cup ground flaxseed

1 teaspoon ground cardamom

3 ripe bananas, mashed (about 1½ cups)

Simple and wholesome, cardamom has a flavor and fragrance all its own. The addition of the ground flaxseed, full of omega-3s, makes this one of the healthiest sweets you can eat. Cardamom is used to spice both sweet and savory dishes and is found in Indian and Middle Eastern cuisines. It comes as whole pods, seeds, or ground. It has a strong, sweet, pungent flavor and aroma, with hints of lemon and mint. If you don't want to invest in this spice, you can substitute equal parts cinnamon and ginger powder, or cinnamon and ground cloves. Or just use cinnamon.

1. Preheat the oven to 350°F. Line a baking sheet with parchment paper.

2. In a small bowl, place the dates and cover with hot water. Let sit until softened, 10 to 30 minutes, depending on the dates, and then drain. Purée in a food processor or blender. Set the date paste aside.

3. In the food processor, grind the oats and ground flaxseed until they resemble flour.

4. In a large bowl, mix together the cardamom and mashed bananas. Stir in the ground oat-flaxseed mixture.

continued →

Cardamom Date Bites *continued*

5. Form into walnut-size balls and flatten a little. Place on the baking sheet and form an indentation in the middle using a ¼ teaspoon measuring spoon. Fill each indentation with about ½ teaspoon of date paste.

6. Bake 15 minutes or until the bites are golden.

Leftovers: Store in an airtight container for up to 3 days.

Per serving (1 cookie): Calories: 82; Fat: 2g; Saturated fat: 0g; Carbohydrate: 16g; Fiber: 3g; Sugar: 7g; Protein: 2g; Iron: 1mg; Sodium: 3mg

Measurements and Conversions

VOLUME EQUIVALENTS (LIQUID)

US STANDARD	US STANDARD (OUNCES)	METRIC (APPROXIMATE)
2 tablespoons	1 fl. oz.	30 mL
¼ cup	2 fl. oz.	60 mL
½ cup	4 fl. oz.	120 mL
1 cup	8 fl. oz.	240 mL
1½ cups	12 fl. oz.	355 mL
2 cups or 1 pint	16 fl. oz.	475 mL
4 cups or 1 quart	32 fl. oz.	1 L
1 gallon	128 fl. oz.	4 L

OVEN TEMPERATURES

FAHRENHEIT	CELSIUS (APPROXIMATE)
250°F	120°C
300°F	150°C
325°F	165°C
350°F	180°C
375°F	190°C
400°F	200°C
425°F	220°C
450°F	230°C

VOLUME EQUIVALENTS (DRY)

US STANDARD	METRIC (APPROXIMATE)
⅛ teaspoon	0.5 mL
¼ teaspoon	1 mL
½ teaspoon	2 mL
¾ teaspoon	4 mL
1 teaspoon	5 mL
1 tablespoon	15 mL
¼ cup	59 mL
⅓ cup	79 mL
½ cup	118 mL
⅔ cup	156 mL
¾ cup	177 mL
1 cup	235 mL
2 cups or 1 pint	475 mL
3 cups	700 mL
4 cups or 1 quart	1 L

WEIGHT EQUIVALENTS

US STANDARD	METRIC (APPROXIMATE)
½ ounce	15 g
1 ounce	30 g
2 ounces	60 g
4 ounces	115 g
8 ounces	225 g
12 ounces	340 g
16 ounces or 1 pound	455 g

References

American Heart Association. "The Skinny on Fats." Last modified April 30, 2017. https://www.heart.org/en/health-topics/cholesterol/prevention-and-treatment-of-high-cholesterol-hyperlipidemia/the-skinny-on-fats.

Animal Clock. Accessed June 2019. https://animalclock.org.

Berry, Jennifer. "What Are the Benefits of Chlorophyll?" *Medical News Today.* June 2019. https://www.medicalnewstoday.com/articles/322361.php.

Bildirici, Lottie. "Running, Chia Seeds and an Incredible Trip with the Tarahumara People." *Women's Running Magazine.* May 30, 2017. https://www.womensrunning.com/2017/05/nutrition/tarahumara-people-chia-seeds_75369.

Bjarnadottir, Adda. "6 Evidence-Based Health Benefits of Hemp Seeds." Healthline. September 11, 2018. https://www.healthline.com/nutrition/6-health-benefits-of-hemp-seeds.

Blue Zones. "Okinawa, Japan. Secrets of the World's Longest-Living Women." May 2018. https://www.bluezones.com/exploration/okinawa-japan/.

Campbell, T. Colin and Thomas Campbell. *The China Study: The Most Comprehensive Study of Nutrition Ever Conducted and the Startling Implications for Diet, Weight Loss, and Long-Term Health.* Dallas, TX: BenBella Books, Inc., 2006.

Campbell, T. Colin. "Dairy Protein Causes Cancer." T. Colin Campbell Center for Nutrition Studies. December 10, 2014. https://nutritionstudies.org/provocations-dairy-protein-causes-cancer/.

Campbell, T. Colin. "Dr. Campbell's Recommendations for Dietary Guidelines." T. Colin Campbell Center for Nutrition Studies. May 2015. https://nutritionstudies.org/2015-dietary-guidelines-commentary/.

Cassileth, Barrie. "Lycopene." *Cancer Network, Home of Journal Oncology.* March 22, 2010. https://www.cancernetwork.com/integrative-oncology/lycopene/

Climate Nexus. "Animal Agriculture's Impact on Climate Change." https://climatenexus.org/climate-issues/food/animal-agricultures-impact-on-climate-change/.

De Vogel, Johan, Denise Jonker-Termont, Esther van Lieshout, Martijn Katan, and Roelof van der Meer. "Green Vegetables, Red Meat and Colon Cancer: Chlorophyll Prevents the Cytotoxic and Hyperproliferative Effects of Haem in Rat Colon." *Carcinogenesis* 26, no. 2 (February 2005): 387–93. doi:10.1093/carcin/bgh331.

Delimaris, Ioannis. "Adverse Effects Associated with Protein Intake above the Recommended Dietary Allowance for Adults." *ISRN Nutrition* (July 2013). doi:10.5402/2013/126929.

Environmental Working Group. "Meat Eater's Guide to Climate Change + Health." September 2019. https://www.ewg.org/meateatersguide/.

Esselstyn Jr., C.B. "Why Does the Diet Eliminate Oil Entirely?" May 2018. http://www.dresselstyn.com/site/why-does-the-diet-eliminate-oil-entirely/.

Food and Agriculture Organization of the United Nations. "Key Facts and Findings—By the Numbers: GHG Emissions by Livestock." August 2019. http://www.fao.org/news/story/en/item/197623/icode/.

Forgrieve, Janet. "The Growing Acceptance of Veganism." *Forbes*. November 2, 2018. https://www.forbes.com/sites/janetforgrieve/2018/11/02/picturing-a-kindler-gentler-world-vegan-month/#11bc759a2f2b.

Forks Over Knives. Documentary. May 2011. https://www.forksoverknives.com.

GlobalData. "Top Trends in Prepared Foods 2017: Exploring Trends in Meat, Fish and Seafood; Pasta, Noodles and Rice; Prepared Meals; Savory Deli Food; Soup; and Meat Substitutes." GlobalData Top Trends series. June 2017. https://www.globalmarketanalyst.com/samples/820592/Top-Trends-in-Prepared-Foods-2017-Exploring-trends-in-meat-fish-and-seafood-pasta-noodles-and-rice-prepared-meals-savory-deli-food-soup-and-meat-substitutes.

Good Food Institute. "Plant-Based Market Overview." April 2019. https://www.gfi.org/marketresearch.

Greger, Michael. "Changing Protein Requirements." Nutrition Facts. April 11, 2019. https://nutritionfacts.org/2019/04/11/changing-protein-requirements/.

Greger, Michael. "The Great Protein Fiasco." Nutrition Facts. June 27, 2016. https://nutritionfacts.org/video/the-great-protein-fiasco/.

Harvard T.H. Chan School of Public Health. "The Nutrition Source: Protein." May 2018. https://www.hsph.harvard.edu/nutritionsource/what-should-you-eat /protein/.

Harvard T.H. Chan School of Public Health. "The Nutrition Source: Straight Talk About Soy." June 2019. https://www.hsph.harvard.edu/nutritionsource/soy/.

Hewlings, Susan and Douglas Kalman. "Curcumin: A Review of Its Effects on Human Health." *Foods* 6, no. 10 (October 22, 2017): 92. doi:10.3390/foods6100092.

Jardine, Meghan. "Seven Reasons to Keep Saturated Fat Off Your Plate." Physicians Committee for Responsible Medicine. November 5, 2018. https://www.pcrm .org/news/blog/seven-reasons-keep-saturated-fat-your-plate.

Levine, Morgan, Jorge A. Suarez, Sebastian Brandhorst, Pinchas Cohen, Eileen M. Crimmins, Valter D. Longo, et al. "Low Protein Intake Is Associated with a Major Reduction in IGF-1, Cancer, and Overall Mortality in the 65 and Younger but Not Older Population." *Cell Metabolism* 19, no. 3 (March 2014): 407–17. doi:10.1016 /j.cmet.2014.02.006.

McClees, Heather. "Are We Eating Too Much Protein? A Scientist Makes the Connection Between Protein and Cancer." One Green Planet. January 2016. https:// www.onegreenplanet.org/news/t-colin-campbell-protein-and-cancer/

Metges, Cornelia C. and Christian Barth. "Metabolic Consequences of a High Dietary-Protein Intake in Adulthood: Assessment of the Available Evidence." *The Journal of Nutrition* 130, 4 (April 2000): 886–89.

Oliveira, Rosane. "Why Olive Oil Is Not Healthy for Your Heart." *Forks Over Knives.* February 14, 2018. https://www.forksoverknives.com/why-olive-oil-is-not-healthy -for-your-heart/#gs.ff3te0.

Ornish, Dean. "The Myth of High-Protein Diets." *The New York Times.* March 23, 2015. https://www.nytimes.com/2015/03/23/opinion/the-myth-of-high-protein -diets.html.

Panche, A. N., A. D. Diwan, and S. R. Chandra. "Flavonoids: An Overview." *Journal of Nutritional Science* (December 29, 2016): e47. doi:10.1017/jns.2016.41.

Physicians Committee for Responsible Medicine. "There Is No Safe Amount of Processed Meat." April 2019. https://www.pcrm.org/good-nutrition/nutrition -information/processed-meat.

Physicians Committee for Responsible Medicine. "Health Concerns About Dairy: Avoid the Dangers of Dairy with a Plant-Based Diet" April 2019. https://www.pcrm.org/good-nutrition/nutrition-information/health-concerns-about-dairy.

Ramos, Sonia, María Angeles Martin, and Luis Goya. "Effects of Cocoa Antioxidants in Type 2 Diabetes Mellitus." *Antioxidants (Basel)* 6, no. 4 (December 2017): 84. doi:10.3390/antiox6040084.

Science Daily. "Fruit and Vegetables May Be Important for Mental as Well as Physical Well-Being." February 5, 2019. https://www.sciencedaily.com/releases/2019/02/190205144450.htm/.

Slavin, Joanne and Beate Lloyd. "Health Benefits of Fruits and Vegetables." *Advances in Nutrition* 3, no. 4 (July 2012): 506–16. doi:10.3945/an.112.002154.

Song, Mingyang, Teresa T. Fung, Frank B. Hu, Walter C. Willett, Valter D. Longo, Andrew T. Chan, and Edward L. Giovannucci. "Association of Animal and Plant Protein Intake with All-Cause and Cause-Specific Mortality." *JAMA Internal Medicine* 176, no. 10 (October 2016):1453–463. doi:10.1001/jamainternmed.2016.4182.

T. Colin Campbell Center for Nutrition Studies. "A History of The China Study." https://nutritionstudies.org/the-china-study/.

World Health Organization. "Protein and Amino Acid Requirements in Human Nutrition." WHO Technical Report Series. January 2007. https://www.who.int/nutrition/publications/nutrientrequirements/WHO_TRS_935/en/.

World Health Organization. "Q&A on the Carcinogenicity of the Consumption of Red Meat and Processed Meat." October 2015. https://www.who.int/features/qa/cancer-red-meat/en/.

Resources

BOOKS

The Cheese Trap: How Breaking a Surprising Addiction Will Help You Lose Weight, Gain Energy, and Get Healthy by Dr. Neal D. Barnard, MD

The China Study by T. Colin Campbell, PhD, and Thomas M. Campbell II, MD

Eating Animals by Jonathan Safran Foer

How Not to Die: Discover the Foods Scientifically Proven to Prevent and Reverse Disease by Dr. Michael Greger, MD, and Gene Stone

How Not to Diet: The Groundbreaking Science of Healthy, Permanent Weight Loss by Dr. Michael Greger, MD

The Joyful Vegan: How to Stay Vegan in a World That Wants You to Eat Meat, Dairy, and Eggs by Colleen Patrick-Goudreau

Living the Farm Sanctuary Life: The Ultimate Guide to Eating Mindfully, Living Longer, and Feeling Better Every Day by Gene Baur and Gene Stone

Peace Is Every Step: The Path of Mindfulness in Everyday Life by Thich Nhat Hanh

The Plant-Based Solution: America's Healthy Heart Doc's Plan to Power Your Health by Joel K. Kahn, MD

Prevent and Reverse Heart Disease: The Revolutionary, Scientifically Proven, Nutrition-Based Cure by Caldwell B. Esselstyn Jr., MD

The Starch Solution: Eat the Foods You Love, Regain Your Health, and Lose the Weight for Good! by John A. McDougall, MD, and Mary McDougall

When Things Fall Apart: Heart Advice for Difficult Times by Pema Chödrön

Whole: Rethinking the Science of Nutrition by T. Colin Campbell, PhD

DOCUMENTARIES

Cowspiracy

Eating Animals

Forks Over Knives

The Game Changers

COOKBOOKS

The Conscious Cook by Tal Ronnen

Crossroads: Extraordinary Recipes from the Restaurant That Is Reinventing Vegan Cuisine by Tal Ronnen

Forks Over Knives: The Plant-Based Way to Health by T. Colin Campbell, PhD, and Caldwell B. Esselstyn Jr., MD

Vedge: 100 Plates Large and Small That Redefine Vegetable Cooking by Rich Landau and Kate Jacoby

NONPROFITS

T. Colin Campbell Center for Nutrition Studies—Nutritionstudies.org

Farm Sanctuary—FarmSanctuary.org

Nutrition Facts—NutritionFacts.org

Sierra Club Foundation—SierraClubFoundation.org

Recipe Index

Index

N

Acknowledgments

Thank you to the Ordinary Vegan health and wellness community. Your emails, messages, and kind words inspire me to work harder every day. I couldn't do any of this without all of you.

Tracey Shaffer Lunn, who steered the Ordinary Vegan ship so that I could devote my time to this book. I am forever grateful.

Thanks also to:

My family, especially my sister, Susan Beck, for always listening and encouraging me.

Barbara Scull and Jenifer Polenzani Benson for your recipe inspiration, support, and friendship.

My California family. I can't imagine life without you.

Dave Stein, my number one fan, for always showing such faith in me.

The A Team—Jenifer Juniper, Debbie Pisaro, and Julie Muncy. Thank you for your sisterhood for more than 25 years.

The boys who make me laugh—Sawyer Wilde Lunn, Truman Young, and Brant Weil.

My recipe tester, Hae Jung Cho. Thanks for your finely honed palate.

Everyone at Callisto Media who made this book a reality.

Written in memory of Barbara Montuori and Esther Hilton.

About the Author

NANCY MONTUORI is the founder of Ordinary Vegan, an online health and wellness community dedicated to a plant-based lifestyle.

Since 2011, Nancy has advocated a plant-based diet for health and wellness, the environment, and animal welfare. A recognized expert on the culinary and health benefits of a vegan diet, Nancy has helped propel plant-based eating into the mainstream.

She shares her recipes and message of health and wellness through her website, social media, TV, radio, magazines, and holistic fitness retreats. She is also the host of the popular vegan podcast *Ordinary Vegan*.

Nancy is continuously busy with a diverse range of projects: constantly testing new recipes, writing her next book, developing innovative cannabidiol (CBD) products, or on the road teaching cooking and nutrition.

Her number one goal is to help people live a long, healthy life that is kind to the environment and protects animals.